SUGARBAKERS
FROM SWEAT TO SWEETNESS

by *Bryan Mawer*

ANGLO-GERMAN FAMILY HISTORY SOCIETY PUBLICATIONS

First edition published in 2007

Sub-editing by Lynn Burling
Design and production by
Rochart, 69 Harlech Road, Abbots Langley, Herts. WD5 0BE

Published by Anglo-German Family History Society Publications
23 Coneydale, Welwyn Garden City, Herts, AL8 7RX, UK.

ISBN 978-0-9547632-3-7

Typeset in Helvetica and Palatino

Contents

List of Illustrations

Preface

Many German immigrants to the United Kingdom worked in particular industries, like pork butchers, hairdressers, furriers, tailors and, possibly the largest group of all: sugarbakers. The Anglo-German Family History Society, soon after it was formed in 1987, published a small booklet by Roy Bernard on sugarbakers, to inform those new members who had discovered that their German immigrant ancestor was a sugarbaker and wanted to know what they did for a living. That booklet was very helpful in its day but has been out of print for many years.

As the Internet evolved, the Society was very pleased to see Bryan Mawer's ever-growing website on sugarbakers, www.mawer.clara.net. So when the Society decided to publish a new book on sugarbakers, to join our growing list of books on "German" occupations in the UK, we were very grateful that Bryan agreed to write it.

Now that the book is ready, I am sure that those of us with sugarbaker ancestors, whether German or not, will find the book invaluable. It will also be of great value to anyone with an interest in the sugar industry. There are no other books that deal with the history of the trade in such depth, and describe the terrible conditions those working in the industry had to endure. It is also a great read!

So, if you have ancestors who were sugar bakers, this is the book for you.

Peter Towey
Vice-President, Anglo-German Family History Society
March 2007

Introduction

Welcome to the world of sugar refining. Not the hugely industrialised, multi-national enterprises of today, but the hot, sweet-smelling, unhealthy processes of the 18th and 19th centuries that killed our ancestors early and changed tall stalks of grass into tiny crystals that made drinks palatable and foods a little tastier. It's probable that you have opened this book because you have found this occupation written against one or more of your early family: on a birth or marriage certificate, in a census, or more worryingly in an inquest report or on a death certificate. I think these are the reasons why most of us have begun to enquire into this little-heard-of occupation, and I hope the following will help to give you a clearer understanding of what these folks did for a living, where they worked and where they lived, and maybe where they originated from.

Quite simply *"sugarbakers"* were those who worked in Britain's sugarhouses or sugar refineries. As the 17th century European sugar industry was dominated by Amsterdam and Hamburg, the name was derived from the Dutch "suikerbakker" and the German "Zuckerbäcker", and it was variously written as sugar baker, sugar-baker, or sugarbaker. The English language had no equivalent word or phrase other than "labourer in a sugarhouse", so the word was not translated from the German but was a German word, brought here by Germans, spoken by Germans, and entered into our language, albeit for a short time, because those who heard it understood it and accepted it without question. "Sugarbaker" is the normal form you'll find in documents written in Britain by those associated with the churches, schools, charities and other organisations within the German communities. I shall use "sugarbaker" throughout this book, except of course in any quotations. In your own research, however, you are likely to find the two-word form used by census enumerators and Anglican clergy, who wrote what they heard using two common English words.

The vast majority of sugarbakers, escaping the lack of employment on the land and the consequent poverty, were unskilled labourers: stoking fires, unloading raw sugar, ladling boiling syrup, pouring bullocks' blood, grinding animal charcoal, cleaning filters, filling moulds with hot sugar, loading ovens, etc. Skilled men were few, usually only the sugar boiler who ran the process and managed the men. In the larger refineries there would have been more than one boiler, but the "secrets" of the process were kept amongst "the few" in the early years. As mechanisation grew, more skilled men were required, but skilled in the management and maintenance of steam engines and specialist machinery rather than how sugar was refined.

"Sugarbaker" was the term used by the migrant German workers to describe themselves, though it was sometimes used to describe other nationalities of refinery workers particularly in London. The British sugar refining industry, by the very nature of the supply of its raw material from overseas, was primarily located in London, Liverpool, Greenock and Bristol, with German labourers predominating in London, sharing the load with the Irish in Liverpool, but being few in Greenock and Bristol. Many other cities and towns had refineries but only Hull, as an entry point for migrants, employed many German workers. The workers lived very close to their workplaces and small migrant communities developed allowing religious and cultural traditions to continue. German churches, schools and charities were set up, and German food, drink and music became part of local life. In *On Duty with Inspector Field*, Charles Dickens describes accompanying the inspector on a tour of public houses and hostelries to the east of the City of London, and says: *"Not that I call the company very select, or the dancing very graceful – even so graceful as that of the German Sugar Bakers, whose assembly, by the Minories, we stopped to visit."*

A little further from the City in the 1860s, Dickens again, in *The Uncommercial Traveller*, writes that he was in Commercial Road, and… *"Pleasantly wallowing in the abundant mud of that thoroughfare, and greatly enjoying the huge piles of buildings belonging to the sugar refiners."* And once accompanying a policeman… *"My beat lying round by Whitechapel Church, and the adjacent sugar-refineries – great buildings, tier upon tier, that have the appearance of being nearly related to the dock-warehouses at Liverpool."* Indeed, from small beginnings, the sugarhouses, as they were often called, developed into huge buildings, their size and design dictated by the processes within. Heat was essential, first generated by open fires, later by steam. Heat permeated the whole building and the whole process, making the working conditions unpleasant to say the least. James Greenwood[1] visited a refinery in 1876 and described watching figures scurrying about that he soon discovered to be men in a condition of at least semi-nudity… and this was when conditions had improved! Today, many complain that Health and Safety at Work has gone too far and is at times restricting production, but these workers had no such protection. Accidents and fatalities

were common, many documented in the newspapers or described in Coroners' reports. *The Times* of 26 November 1891 (which is at the very end of the East End sugar refining era) reports that… *"George Duhn, 61, labourer at Messrs. Martineau's sugar refinery, Christian Street, St George's-in-the-East, [was] discovered lying in a tank of boiling syrup; verdict: accidental death."* Inquests came down on the side of the employers even when, for example, a worker had been crushed to death by a falling roof timber. However, the employers often contributed to collections for the families of the dead or injured and to the charities which supported them.

The sugar refining industry of England and Scotland began in 1544 and for a century or so there were just a few sugarhouses, as has been the case for the last century or so though for very different reasons. I will concentrate this book on those years in between, 1700–1900, when many of our ancestors, whether German or Dutch, Irish or Polish, or simply from "Foreign Parts", were new to this country, and with few exceptions, new to an industry that offered such long hours and appalling conditions that in most cases the indigenous workforce steered clear of it.

"Particles of sugar in their pure state are white; and to present them in this white crystalline form is the object of the sugar refiner." – Dodd[2]

Notes
1 *The Wilds of London* by James Greenwood, 1876.
2 "A Day at a Sugar Refinery" by G. Dodd, *The Penny Magazine* No 582, April 1841.

Who were they?

George F Tutte, foreman at Martineau's, 13 Kingward Street, London, with four of his children, Christmas Day 1946, © Jane E Tutte Mayberry

Herman Almeroth was a German sugarbaker in the Whitechapel area of London from the early 1790s to his death in 1812. Born around 1762 we know not where, married in London, had seven children of whom four died in infancy, eventually set up his own small sugarhouse and worked himself into an early grave – all probably rather familiar to other researchers of the same trade.

Many years later, John Adamson, Martin Besnisco, Thomas Bowden, Henry Dorning, Pious Lascowitch, Peter Rasmussen, David Steven, Christian Tick, William Tobin, and Frederick Wellins all appeared in the 1881 census. All were sugarbakers in one or other of the refineries still working in England and Scotland. All were married, six of them to local women, and all had young families. All but two were in their 30s, and four of them had lodgers to help pay the bills. Most importantly though, all had left their birthplaces, their communities and their families in Sweden, Russia, Wales, Devon,

Poland, Denmark, Scotland, Germany, Ireland, and Prussia respectively. Like Herman, it's unlikely that any of them brought with them any skills of the trade, but simply their muscle and their willingness to work. This is not a cross-section of the workforce, far from it, as different locations were dominated by different nationalities, but it does show that labourers were just labourers and, provided they could get there, the refineries appear to have welcomed them.

This is not to say there was no local labour; some towns and cities used more than others. There are few employee lists or company records available. Perhaps they went the way of those of Fairrie & Co Ltd, one of the largest refineries in Liverpool, who resolved that after the winding up of the company was completed in 1931 the books and documents of the company should be destroyed.[1] Early photographs of both Lyle's[2] & Tate's[3] in Silvertown provide late but important detail. It is the censuses of 1841 to

8

1901 that help us to work out the nationalities of the later workers, and in some cases the exact refineries in which they worked. These are invaluable for family research, often providing a specific birthplace.

Whilst the mid- to late-19th century is the easiest period in which to research sugarbakers, and where many researchers first stumble across the occupation, we need to go back at least two centuries to understand the importance of the migrant worker to the industry.

In 1666 the Great Fire of London was started by a baker of bread, although it could just as easily have been started by a sugarbaker or a worker in any of the trades operating at the time given the construction of the buildings, the working conditions, and the use of open fires as sources of heat. Sugar refining had begun in London just over a hundred years earlier, and though records are few, Cornelius Bossigne and Fernando Poyns are named amongst those who are reputed to have started the industry. Stow[4], the historian and mapmaker, says that, *"About the year 1544 refining of sugar was first used in England. There were but two sugar-houses; and the profit was little, by reason there were so many sugar-bakers in Antwerp and thence better and cheaper than it could be afforded in London"*. Similarly, in Bristol the single refinery of Robert Aldworth, and later Giles Elbridge, set against St Peter's Church, had begun in 1612, but was not joined by other refineries for some 40 years. The London trade grew slowly, mostly in the City, though there is evidence of sugarhouses, probably established by George Monck or William Pritchard, at Woolwich on the estate of Tower Place, bought in 1676 by King Charles II for the building of what we know today as Woolwich Arsenal.[5] After the Great Fire, Allyn Smith, a prominent London refiner, with Richard Cleveland and Daniel Danvers, began refining in Liverpool, and at a similar time sugarhouses were established in Glasgow.

The first two Glasgow sugarhouses appear to have been established by groups of local businessmen who, without expert knowledge of the sugar refining process,

employed foreign refiners to run the day-to-day workings of the refineries. Deerr[6] tells us that the Eastern Sugar House *"employed a German to be master boiler, and the project proved effectual, so that their stock wonderfully increased"*. This German was Zacharius Zebbes, born about 1644 in Rostock, Germany, who learnt the sugar refining trade in Amsterdam, and was probably appointed at the start of the business in 1669. Zebbes died ten years later, aged about 35, having amassed, by the standards of the day, quite a fortune. In his will[7] he left legacies to some of the partners of the business as well as his barber, his servant, and the women who nursed him throughout his illness. He listed debts owed him by the business, and instructed the partners to pay some of that money to the poor of the church. The residue of his estate, more than £2000 Scots money, he left to the poor of the Merchant Hospital in Glasgow, and Glasgow Museums have a board commemorating this act of generosity. This is probably a museum copy of the original board, possibly originally at the Merchants House, but it shows the sum to be £2277 - 9s - 6d Scots money. The board reads… *"Zacharias Zebbes. Shugar boyller in the Eister Shugarie of Gllasgow was born in the town of Rwstike in Germanie, departid this Lyf in Glasgow December 1679, abowt the 36 yeir of his age and left of Legasie to the Poor of this Howse, 2277 lib, 09 sh, 06 d, Scots."*, and this is confirmed in the records of The Merchants House, Glasgow.

Similarly, in Bristol in 1665, Godfrey von Itterne from Hamburg was employed by Thomas Ellis as his technical expert at the Whitson Court Sugar House. He sought and obtained naturalisation in 1666–7. He died a rich man in 1686; his will[8] mentioning his wife Abigail and six children, as well as his friends, most of whom were in the same or similar business to himself. He also left money to the poor of certain parishes in the city.

So, nearing the end of the 17th century, four of the kingdom's major cities were producing sugar. The tea and coffee that had become so popular had to have something to sweeten them, and it was from this time that the industry would develop to its prime in the first half of the 19th century. The consumption of sugar in the UK increased from 4 lb a head a year in 1700 to 18 lb a head a year in 1800.[9]

There was by now a ready supply of raw sugar arriving from across the Atlantic thanks(?) to a rapidly increasing slave trade. However, a further catalyst that was to give the sugar trade necessary impetus was an unexpected one… the death of Queen Anne, and the end of the Stuart line. With no heir to the throne, the Elector of Hanover became King George I of England in 1714, and the country would be ruled by German kings for more than a century. Not only did George I bring a complete household of staff, but his court relocated to London introducing a whole new breed of bureaucrat, banker, scholar, artist, medical man and businessman. This meant that with time, businessmen always eager for new trade could settle in London and establish their businesses with a certain freedom, and without having to deal with the English bankers.[10]

German and Dutch refiners, who appear to have been deeply secretive about "the art of sugar refining", came over to set up their own sugarhouses, or to run new sugarhouses for London merchants, often in partnership. By 1750, names such as Lilkendey, Ravencamp, Schroder, Burmester, Schutte, Rehme, Rotshouch and Tielhen appeared over the doors of sugarhouses, with many more unidentified sugar boilers developing businesses for their English employers.

Christian Tielhen was refining sugar in 1748, probably in Leman Street, Whitechapel, where he was living at the time of his death in 1761. He married Ann Hart in 1750, and their two children, Edward and Mary, were baptised in 1751 and 1753 respectively.[11] From his will[12] it would appear that Ann and Mary died before Christian, leaving Edward, aged 10, to inherit all. Edward was apprenticed to Thomas Sowerby, a musician, in 1766.[13]

Christian Tielhen's will gives no indication of his wealth, but the sale catalogue for the auction of his belongings[14] shows his lifestyle to have been a good one – a large house in Leman Street probably adjacent to the sugarhouse, mahogany and walnut furniture, an eight-day clock, Venetian printed curtains, thirty pairs of sheets, clothing which included many coats, waistcoats and breeches, wigs, and riding apparel, a well-equipped kitchen and brewhouse, and over fifty books.

There are so very few documents surviving from any era regarding individual businesses that the "Refining Book" Christian Tielhen used to record the sugar produced and to whom it was sold for the short period 1758–60, along with an early "Receipt Book" and letters 1748–51, and a "Bills Delivered Book" 1759–60, are possibly unique documents from that time.[15] They are available to us because some 10 years after Tielhen's death the joint executors of his will, John Arney and Joseph Hess, both sugar refiners, fell into dispute and a box of Tielhen's documents and money which had been kept by Hess was required for the case heard in Chancery.[16]

Tielhen's sugarhouse was averaging about 10 tons (200 cwt) of finished product per boiling, and each boiling took about 2 weeks. Most products were sold some 6–8 weeks after being made, and tax appears to have been paid on the weight of sugar sold rather than the amount it was sold for. In early 1760 he was making sales of around £900 per month.

All three of these books show that Tielhen was not only selling finished, refined sugar products to businesses and individual customers but also to other refiners, and the receipt book shows a variety of men signing on behalf of the company – John Strutt, Charles Abbott, John Mackelean, John Camden, John Tomlinson, Thomas Moore, Stephen Burman, Robert Taylor, Gabriel Hesse and W. Williams; of these the names of Camden, Hesse and Mackelean are known refiners in later years, giving us reason to believe they were learning the trade with Tielhen.

Letters from Germany dated 1751 were addressed to Mr Chr Tielhen, Gingerbread Baker, Round Court in the Strand, London, though detail in his receipt book suggest he had changed occupation well before 1748. Local letters of the same period were addressed to The Wheat Sheaf, New Round Court in the Strand, and these are mainly personal ones and household bills, along with a Sun Insurance policy for the property in Leman Street. The few German letters appear to be from the same person, a friend called Stahne of Wildeshausen, about 20km west of Bremen in Oldenburg. One, written 5 January 1751, thanks him for money sent, talks of a cattle plague in Wildeshausen and of the death of the Queen of Denmark, and asks *"whether Mr Ehlers could send some delicious English honey cake; a Bremen shipmaster could bring it to Bremen and give it to Herr Simmis."*

By the time Christian Tielhen died in 1761 the sugar refining trade was thriving. There were said to be about 80 sugarhouses in London, at least 20 in Bristol,[17] maybe 8 in Liverpool, 3 or 4 in Glasgow, a couple in Chester, and one each in Lancaster, Sheffield, Hull, Whitehaven and Southampton. Within four years the Clyde trade would become established in Greenock, with its better access for shipping, and this small town would soon be a major rival to Bristol and Liverpool.

The only sources of information regarding the industry, and the people that ran it and worked in it up to this time, are archived documents and the one or two histories written since. The documents are wide-ranging, from business records to land deals, from apprentice lists[18] to insurance records, from marriage settlements to wills; it is just a pity there was no Sugarbakers Guild. The introduction around this time of regular trade directories, listing both individuals and businesses, allows us, with far greater certainty, to work out where the refineries were and who owned them.

These show that much of London's refining was still being carried out within the City. There were a number of sugarhouses in Whitefriars, but most were along the length of Upper Thames Street and the narrow streets around St Paul's, with the coopers and brokers working in the small area of Great Tower Street, Mark Lane and Mincing Lane between London Bridge and The Tower. Next to the notorious Fleet River, an open sewer until it was covered in 1766, stood 26 Water Lane, Blackfriars, where one of the most influential German figures in the London trade, Harman

Samler, could be found. There is evidence of him having working premises in this area as far back as 1749,[19] however he obtained a substantial property from the widow Sikes and her son John in 1758 on a lease for seven years at an annual rent of £40.[20] It comprised a dwelling house, timber yard, sugar millhouse, and stables as follows…

In the room two pairs of stairs forward – one closet with shelves round it with a door and two iron hinges a wood chimney piece set with black and white tiles and five old marble squares. The dining [room] up one pair of stairs forward – a wood chimney piece with a stone hearth set with galley tiles five grey marble squares edged with black marble a Beaufort painted and guilt compleat with doors hinges and proper fastenings a cupboard under the same with a shelf and double doors with iron hinges and locks and keys to two doors. In the little room forwards up one pair of stairs – a fireplace set with galley tiles a fire stone and marble slab piers. In the little room forwards up one pair of stairs – a lock and key to the door. In the little parlour on the ground floor – a stone chimney piece hearth and fire stone and set with galley tiles two small cupboards with shelves doors hinges locks. In the scullery – a wood sink compleat lined with lead with an oak stand fixed in the wall for water tub two shelves. In the kitchen an open deal dresser complete with three shelves over it a dark closet with a door and iron hinges a fireplace with stone slab a wooden chimney piece with one shelf and two racks a cupboard with one shelf a dresser over the door with four shelves round it. In the cellar – the water laid into the cellar and up into the scullery with brass cocks and leaden pipe and leaden waste pipe from the scullery into the sink in the cellar a door to the cellar stairs with two iron hinges an iron latch and two iron bolts. In the yard next Fleet Ditch – the stable complete with roof covered with pantiles and painted a rack and manger and hay loft a door to the Ditch side with an iron bolt and staples and one pair of iron hinges the stable paved with cobbles and a door and stout lock and a pair of iron hinges dimensions of the stable and hay loft thirty seven foot five inches long out to out fourteen foot wide nineteen foot high the back front and fifteen foot high the fore front. A sugar millhouse next Water Lane in the front fifteen foot eight inches wide twenty two foot seven inches deep and twelve foot high the front part weather boarded and two folding doors with two pair of hinges and proper fastenings and the back front weather boarded and covered with pantiles and painted a girder and joysts and part boarded on the raising plates an open door to the passage next Water Lane with iron hinges and a stout lock and key. The front of the yard next Fleet Ditch inclosed twenty nine foot wide ten foot high with a large bressummer and seven posts and two close doors and three open doors with iron hinges and proper fastenings. A necessary house complete with a door iron hinges and proper fastenings. The foot way in the yard paved with free stone and lead pipe from the top of the house to the first floor to run away the water from there.

The records of the Sun Fire Office[21] show that Samler, and his sons Richard and William who succeeded him, insured with them sugarhouses in Holland Street, Puddle Dock and St Andrew's Hill, all in Blackfriars and later Angel Alley in Whitechapel. This is rather ironic as Harman Samler was a leading force in the founding of the Phoenix Fire Office in 1782. It was founded initially by sugar refiners for sugar refiners, and prompted by objections to the excessive rates charged by the existing insurance companies. Samler was the first of three Company

Harman Samler , © Paul Steinmetz

signatories on the very first policy issued, that being to Messrs Bourdorff and Schwenck whose sugarhouse was situated in Mill Bank Street in the Parish of St John the Evangelist, Westminster.[22]

When Harman Samler died in 1792, the notice in *The Times* read... *"On Saturday morning, after a few hours' illness, died at his house on Clapham Common, HARMAN SAMLER, Esq., an eminent Sugar Refiner of this City, and one of the Directors of the Phoenix Fire Office. His exemplary life and character, which obtained the esteem and affection of all who knew him, deserve particular mention at this time; by the most exact probity and unwearied application, he acquired a large fortune; he was pious, charitable, unassuming, a kind husband, a fond father, and a warm friend."* His will[23] was proved in the same year, leaving his dwelling house and 3 1/2 acres on the south side of Clapham Common, his sugarhouses and messuages, at least £70,000 and his Phoenix shares to his wife and six children, having already settled more than £10,000 on his children in preceding years.

At this time aliens living and working in Britain, particularly merchants and businessmen, had lower status in the commercial world than the British and, to overcome this, needed a grant of denization or naturalisation. Harman Samler received a grant of denization in 1767, with an address at St Ann, Blackfriars.[24] Lists of denizations and naturalisations can be found at The National Archives (TNA) and, where supporting documents are available, these often include details of origin, family, occupation and religion. In 1851, Lear Wrede, a sugar refiner in Greenock married to a British woman and having nine children, seven of whom were still living, sought and was granted naturalisation. His application included "memorials" from the minister of his church, the Procurator Fiscal, two bankers, and his father-in-law. He had been born in Hanover in 1808, arrived in London in 1824 where he worked as a sugar refiner, moved to Greenock in 1832 and married in 1834, being a member of the Established Church of Scotland.[25] Over the years, Lear Wrede ran a number of refineries in Greenock both as partner and sole proprietor, and died in 1874.

Someone who did not need a grant of naturalisation was Reggie Holthouse. He had been born in England but in April 1945, as a rifleman on active service, found himself within a few miles of the small town of Bücken just south of Hoya in northern Germany. He obtained leave for the day, borrowed a bicycle and set off for the town. He found slight damage to the church and the school from German artillery fire, and two houses had been burnt down, but otherwise the town was a pleasant one and there were even other visitors to the church. Reggie was disappointed to find that the pastor was away for the day and would not be returning until after the time at which he would have to return to camp. He was further disappointed when the pastor's wife told him that the church records had all been buried in the ground for safe keeping, and that he would be unable to see the baptism entry for his three times great grandfather. He then found time, on 12 April, to write about his day out in a letter to his uncle Edwin Holthouse back home in Surrey.[26] Reggie Holthouse had hoped to look at the original written records of his family that his uncle Edwin, a surgeon and eye specialist, had so painstakingly researched over the years. Thanks to Edwin Holthouse, the family genealogy is very well documented and can be found in the Holthouse Collection at Northamptonshire Record Office (NRO), the detail of which shows us the closeness of the German sugar refining community in both Germany and London.

It was Carsten Holthouse, born 1738 in Nordholz, son of Johann and grandson of Cord, who came to London to set up in business as a sugar refiner in Wellclose Square, initially it is thought with his brother Christian, and certainly later with Carsten Dirs. There is no mention of whether he brought his skills with him from Germany, although the family had already inter-married with the Ahlers, Dirs, Ehlers and Engelken families in the Bücken area. Following Carsten's marriage to the daughter of another Wellclose Square refiner, Joachim Frederick Dolge in 1778, it would soon have further

close family and business ties to other refining families in London – Batger, Dirs, Engelke, Lilkendey, Mertens, Witte and, in less happy circumstances, Detmar.

Carsten Holthouse died in 1800 and his son, Carsten II, followed his father's trade. In or about 1805 he went into partnership with William Detmar in the business of sugar refining at premises in Bath Terrace on Back Lane, and later in Breezers Hill and Virginia Street, until William's death in 1824. Carsten Holthouse II married about 1809, and in 1816 leased residential property in Upper Edmonton, borrowing capital from Sophia Dirs. In 1823 he extended the lease on the property and, from the events following William Detmar's untimely death, it is clear that he was over-extending himself financially. William Detmar of Upton, Essex, died aged 38, July 1824, leaving a widow Mary Anne, and no will. Over the next couple of years, the full extent of Carsten's financial plight was brought to light. He owed the estate of William Detmar over £10,000. He borrowed and mortgaged further, and relinquished his interests in all the business premises in order

Carsten Holthouse II, © Northamptonshire Record Office, ref: HOLT 622.[29]

to pay his debts. This done, Mary Ann Detmar immediately leased back to him the sugarhouse in Back Lane at £386 per annum. During 1830 the refinery was destroyed by fire. With the help of the insurance money, Carsten rebuilt it, installing the very latest steam equipment at great expense, and so increasing the value of the property;[27] however, he went bankrupt in 1833.[28] Carsten Holthouse II had five sons by his first marriage – a surgeon, a lawyer and a vicar whose own children, in turn, appear to have followed these same professions, and two others who emigrated to Australia.

From 1839 to 1851 the trade directories listed him as a sugar broker at 84 Great Tower Street. Widowed in 1844, he married again in 1849 and some years later moved to Bath where he became a wine merchant. He died in 1864 aged 82.

Little did Carsten Holthouse senior know when he arrived in London that his descendants would permeate the professional classes of English society, but it would appear that his will to succeed was passed on to them. Even Reggie, some 4 or 5 generations later and in a foreign country, was determined to take advantage of the situation in which he found himself.

Bücken is located just west of the River Weser, about 24 miles south east of Bremen and 38 miles north west of Hanover. It falls a few miles south of an area referred to by Horst Rössler as the *Elbe-Weser-Dreieck,*

a roughly triangular area bounded by the rivers Elbe in the east and Weser in the west, and the cities of Hamburg and Bremen. Whilst we can identify sugarbakers arriving in Britain from most parts of Germany,[30] with a fair number from Hessen, by far the most came from this area of Northern Germany. "Hanover" in the census returns usually refers to this area rather than to the city itself, and often a village or town is also mentioned.

Researching numerous sources in both Germany and Britain, Horst Rössler writes,[32]

The majority of German migrants who ended up in the British sugar industry were Hanoverians coming from a restricted, geographically demarcated territory, the so-called Elbe-Weser-Dreieck. Sandwiched in between the two urban centres of Bremen and Hamburg, this was a rural area largely untouched by the industrial

Elbe-Weser-Dreieck, District (Landdrostei) of Stade, Kingdom of Hanover, with bailiwicks (Amtsbezirke), seats of bailiffs (Amtssitze) and places of origin of migrants to UK. (map by Thomas Fock based on an original by Henry Lange, 1859) [31]

revolution that began to transform German society from the 1840s onwards. Actually, throughout the 19th century this region was dominated by dozens of small villages, with the majority of its people making a living from agricultural work, and as many others were seamen this left only a small minority owning small shops or engaging in artisan trades such as tailoring, shoemaking and building.

Between roughly 1750 and the early 1880s, i.e. for several generations, migrants from the Elbe-Weser-Dreieck headed for Britain in search of work in the sugar industry, and as a result of chain migration this Hanoverian territory was linked with certain cities in Britain. The migrants concentrated in particular neighbourhoods of London and Liverpool where they clustered in the streets near the refineries – in the East End of London (e.g. Rupert Street, Pennington Street, Denmark Street, Pell Street, St George's Street and Christian Street) and in the northern part of Liverpool (e.g. Great Mersey Street, Ascot Street, Athol Street, Epson Street and Hopwood Street).

Through networks based on family, relatives and fellow countrymen from Hanover (Elbe-Weser-Dreieck), immigrants who were already living and working in London or Liverpool took care that the newcomers either found lodgings in company-owned dwellings (widespread in London) or provided them with board and lodgings in their rented houses. As census returns show, almost all sugarbaker families had from two to seven subtenants. Among the latter were hardly any British but the lodgers were overwhelmingly Germans from the Elbe-Weser-Dreieck; they were single men aged 20 to 35 and they were workers in the sugar industry.

This migration process, spanning some 150 years, led to the existence of a wide variety of small German communities in Britain, based mainly on origin and occupation rather than large ethnic gatherings. In total, the number of German migrants was never as large as might be thought with only around 28,644 in 1861[33] within a total population of more than 20 million[34] for England and Wales… some 0.14%.

There were varied reasons why these young men should decide to leave their homelands and families, whether temporarily or permanently. Merchants, just like today, would have seen opportunities to expand their businesses or begin new ones, but those of the labouring classes, maybe experiencing an inheritance system in which they saw their father's small farm going to their eldest brother, or simply finding reduced opportunities for work on the land, found it necessary to seek work wherever they could. The attraction of a liberal system of Government compared to that experienced in 19th century Germany may also have been a factor.[35]

Although many settled here permanently and always had the opportunity to become British citizens, some retained their strong German sympathies. Henry Tate's first sugar boiler at his Love Lane refinery in Liverpool in 1872 was Ernest Wedekind, a German who served the company for some 40 years before his outspoken views immediately prior to WWI led to him being interned as an enemy alien. He died in internment.[36]

Many migrants from Germany at that time went to North America, with its rapid growth and supposedly wider opportunities. The reason I mention this is because it is always a good idea for North American researchers of German names to search the British records if they have years missing from their family history. Migration from Germany was not necessarily a direct passage, nor did it always take place over a few months. We know that Britain was a stopping-off point for many on their way to North America. Sometimes it was to change ship as a much larger vessel would be required to cross the Atlantic than to cross the Channel, but often to earn money to pay for the transatlantic leg of their voyage. Many entered at London or Hull with the expressed intention of earning their passage to North America in the sugar industries in London or Liverpool, many sailing from Liverpool.

Heinrich and Christoph Wittekind migrated from Germany to New York arriving in 1871 and 1869 respectively. The exact detail of their birthplace was not recorded in America, but these gentlemen had, however, lived and worked as sugarbakers in London for some years. It would appear that probably the only record outside Germany of their birthplace, Hadamar in Hessen, is in the registers of St George's German Lutheran Church, Alie Street, London, which show the baptisms of their children from 1856 to 1862. Perhaps it took 10–15 years to save enough money to pay for them and their families to cross the Atlantic.

Occasionally it took until the second generation for the migration across the Atlantic to take place. John Herman Mollenhauer was married to Mary Ann Martyn at St Mary Whitechapel, London in 1803, at least four children were born, and then between 1808 and 1812 the family moved to Liverpool where at least two more children were added.[37] Perhaps John had intended to sail to America himself or maybe he just thought business would be better in Liverpool. It was probably he who was refining in Greenfield Street and Oldhall Street with Henry Morgenstern in the early 1820s and a few years later alone in Dale Street.[38] It was his son Henry, born 1812, who eventually made the journey, though the circumstances were somewhat unusual. In 1843, Henry and his brother Richard lived in Cazneau Street and had separate refineries in Naylor Street and Smithfield Street,[39] but sometime before 1851 he joined the Church of the Latter-day Saints and was recruited as the "sugar making expert" in the hugely expensive, though fatally flawed, first attempt by the Church to grow and refine sugar locally in Utah.

Church Elder John Taylor, on a visit to England told Church members at a conference in Manchester, *"We need sugar; the sisters won't like to get along without their tea – I care nothing about it without sugar myself. How must we get that? We are going to raise [sugar] beets as they do in France."* – and therein lay the problem. Extensive research was done in north east France where sugar beet was grown and processed. The machinery and expertise was obtained in Liverpool where sugar was refined from sugar cane, however, and the extraction and initial boiling processes for each are very different.

Fawcett, Preston & Co. Ltd, Phoenix Foundry, Liverpool, supplied all the machinery ordered for the new sugarhouse in

Utah, and Joseph Vernon, an engineer of theirs from Hull, was to go out and install it. Henry Mollenhauer recruited two Liverpool sugar boilers, John Bollwinkle of Germany and Ebnor Connor of Ireland, to go with him. Mollenhauer left his wife and children behind, though the Church promised to pay his wife £1 per week to help with their upkeep. Vernon's wife and younger children did not travel but his son John, an 18 year old sugar worker, made the trip. Bollwinkle took his wife and four children, and Connor took his wife.

The machinery left Liverpool on 6 March 1852 arriving in New Orleans on 26 April; it went up river to St Louis and then more than 1200 miles overland by wagons to Salt Lake City, during the snows of early winter which proved, for the heaviest items, impossible. Some machinery was left by the wayside to be collected in better weather, but even when it did arrive there was no sugarhouse built to accept it. Over the next few years the beet was grown from French seed, the first sugarhouse built and the equipment installed, but there was no way of initially processing the beet to remove the salts nor was there any equipment for producing the necessary animal charcoal required to clarify the sugar. So the small amount of sugar produced was very poor and still tasted of beet. Bollwinkle stayed loyal to the project, but Mollenhauer had left Utah by 1855, and Joseph Vernon left soon after and died some years later in Hawaii.[40] Young John Vernon eventually took himself out into the desert to the south west to farm the land, where he was shot and killed by an Indian; he is buried at Clover. The project was never successful, and sugar would not be produced there until the 1890s.

Ebnor Connor (or Abner as he is listed in the 1851 census) was born in Ireland and was one of the many Irish migrants working in Liverpool, a large number of whom were employed as labourers in the sugar refining industry. They were more often than not called "workers/labourers in a sugarhouse/sugar refinery" rather than sugarbakers, though David McNally is listed in the 1841 census for Glasgow as a "worker in a sugarworks", then

10 years later in the Liverpool census as a "sugar baker". They were just a different nationality working in a different city.

The Irish migrants had a hugely important part to play in the sugar refining industry, particularly in Liverpool and Greenock. They were usually simply referred to as "labourers", and this has since led to an identification problem in the censuses. Where an enumerator has failed to distinguish between the various kinds of labourer by not adding the type or place of work, it is impossible for us to get a true count of those working in the refineries.

There had been a flourishing sugar refining trade in Dublin in the 18th century, with names such as Paumier, Audouin, Villebois, Vignau and Dubedat and Perrier[41] indicating a French influence rather than German. There were fewer sugarhouses in the 1800s. These were not skilled men crossing the Irish Sea but quite probably desperate labourers seeking work and food, escaping the hardships of both the Great Famine in the middle of the century and the eviction of tenant farmers towards either end of it. Like the German migrants, they were farm labourers with no land to work.

Now well into the 19th century we have the great advantage of being able to refer to the census returns for our information. Not only is it often easier to find the origins of these sugar workers, but also we can now separate the owners from the workers, the master boilers from the labourers. We can track sugarbakers through a number of censuses, as well as spot fathers and sons. If we are really lucky we can find the exact refinery where these men worked, either because they were living in company-provided accommodation usually adjacent to the sugarhouse, or because they were living very close to a refinery… they rarely walked far to work!

The Irish migrants are found mostly in Greenock and Liverpool with fewer elsewhere. In 1881 at 74 Ann Street, Greenock, lived a dozen families which included the sugarhouse labourers James Piggott, 32, and his son George, 11, with boarders John Morrell, 23, and Thomas Clark, 21, Samuel Forbes, 61, and son Joseph, 19, John Harran, 23, James Forsyth, 39, and John Moore, 44, and sons Thomas, 22, Samuel, 18, John, 16, and also Alexander, 8, a sugarhouse office boy. Only young George Piggott was born in Greenock, the rest in Ireland. At Earlestown in Lancashire, Irishmen John Coyle and Thomas Gavin both appear in the censuses from 1861 to 1881 working at the Sankey Sugar Works, whilst James Dolan can be traced from 1861, aged 24, to 1901, aged 63, by which time he had graduated from labourer to filterman. In 1851, in St Paul's, Bristol, Timothy Reardon, 41, of Ireland is listed as a sugar refiner along with his sons Timothy, 17, and John, 15, and a lodger, Michael Burke, 22. At the same time brothers Peter Hickey, 38, and James Hickey, 28, both Irishmen and both shown as "sugar bakers", are living at 3 Plummers Row, off Whitechapel Road in London, and James Brown from Galway was an employee at the Glasshouse Street Sugar House.

Of course, like every other refining town and city, Greenock employed some local labour but by the second half of the 19th century the vast majority were Irish. Scottish skills and labour were, however, valued and respected with Scotsmen being employed throughout England. Archibald McGuffie and John Fanco were both working in London in 1851, and John Thomson ran the Sankey Sugar Works at Earlestown from its start-up in 1855. Archibald Houston could not have gone much further without emigrating for he is listed in 1881 as a boiler at the Mill Street Sugar Refinery in Plymouth, though the manager was a local man from Devonport. Many Scotsmen with names such as Fraser, Watson, Anderson and Cameron, were employed in Liverpool, and in 1881 young William Glean, 18, is listed as living in one of the crowded "courts" in Johnson Street.

The 1851 census for London shows that labourers came from Norfolk and Suffolk as well as Colchester, Oxford, Basingstoke and Hull, but by this time only a small proportion of the labour force in the East End was not German. Of the workers that can be identified in the censuses, about 87% of around 1000 workers were German in 1851, but by 1881 the proportion was down to 75% with the total number of workers having declined to around 300, the average age of whom was clearly higher. The Shipping Lists transcribed from TNA HO2 and HO3, 1847–1869, by Len Metzner, show almost 2000 men arriving from Germany who actually stated they were sugarbakers, and there must have been many more who came as labourers and took work in the refineries. Ahrend Huncken of Hanover appears in the censuses of 1851, 1861 and 1871 working at Hall & Boyd's refinery in Breezers Hill, and Herman Schriever of Mehl, Hanover, having lived in Bethnal Green in 1851, is found at 116 Grove Street, St George's in the East, in the 1871, 1881 and 1891 censuses. Contemporary maps show this property to have backed on to the refinery at 6 Christian Street, making it almost certain that Schriever was working for Martineau's. He died aged 77 in early 1897.

Herman Hinrich Evers, whose surname is often spelt with an "A", can be traced through the censuses from age 32 in 1871 to age 63 in 1901. A sugarbaker in all but 1891, when he is listed as a general labourer; always from Germany although Hanover and Bremen are added in 1871 and 1881; and moving from 24 Pell Street to 2 Thomas Court, both in St George's in the East, and then further east to West Ham before 1891. By studying the censuses we can see that Herman and his wife Louise had nine children, with just the one, Claus, following his father's trade. Herman Evers attended St George's German Lutheran Church in Alie Street, the registers of which add much more information. There were 10 children born from 1860 to 1880 with subsequent baptisms, and the addresses read: 62 Leman Street, 18 and then 4 Pell Street, 36 John Street, 24 Pell Street, and 2 Thomas Court. Valuable detail about Herman and Louise is also available; he is listed as a sugarbaker of Warfleth and she as Louise Woldemann or Woltman of Axstedt, both locations in North Germany between Bremen and Bremerhaven. These registers, along with those of the nearby St Paul's German Reformed Church in Hooper Square, are invaluable, often giving much needed information regarding the origins of the

members of their churches. The two churches served the German communities in the East End of London throughout the 19th century, along with the local Anglican parish churches.

Somewhat earlier than the censuses, though far less all-encompassing, church registers began to detail occupations allowing us to pinpoint those who worked in the sugar trade. The parish registers of Sutton-on-Hull show that there were German sugarbakers amongst the parishioners there in the decades either side of 1800 – Peter Warnkin, Daniel Middelstobb, Frederick Schrayder, Daniel Myers and Lear Hendrickson probably worked for Thornton, Watson & Co, or Bassano, Carill & Co, or G F Myers in Hull.

There was indeed a large number of German sugarbakers, but their domination in London and their influence elsewhere, was just too much for some. In 1864 Robert Niccol published an essay[42] describing the state of the industry on Clydeside with detail of the refining processes of the time. He included within this a vehement denunciation of the German refiners, parts of which read…

> … *They [the Germans] are said to have commenced operations in London in 1659, the entire management of English refineries being entrusted into the hands of these foreigners, under whom, in every sense of the term, the British refiner was an absolute slave. The Germans were only to be treated with on certain conditions which, as is reasonable to suppose, were only favourable to themselves, but rather the reverse on the part of their employers, who, having no alternative, were thus obliged to submit to their terms of engagement. The terms entered into between the boiler or practical manager and his employer were, in those days and indeed until a comparatively recent date, in most cases as follows: – Exclusively of a stated salary of some £200 to £300 a-year (more or less, according to the size of the work and other circumstances), and a percentage of the profits of the refiner's business, a free house (the tax burdens on which were paid by the refiner), with other perquisites, as also the exclusive right of employing and dismissing workmen at pleasure.*

… The writer would just remark, in passing, that the Germans who have come to this country from time to time in the capacity of sugar bakers, as they style themselves, have never been known to be accompanied from the Hanseatic towns by their wives and families; but invariably married those of the fair sex belonging to this country, many of whom, in the event of their husbands being obliged to return to their own country, were, with their families, left in a state of abject poverty and wretchedness to become a burden upon our parochial and charitable institutions. This is, in some degree, confirmed by Mr Edwards (author of a history of the West Indies, published in 1793), who… speaks also of "a class of foreigners" (evidently Germans) "employed in English refineries, who live in the most frugal and sparing manner in England, and then return with their savings to their own country." It has likewise been frequently remarked by our countrymen that those foreigners come here in the state of half-clad and half-starved peasants, and after remaining but a short time in this country and working in the refineries here, they soon become more like princes. Some of them have, through their fascinations, even been received into partnership with their employers and not a few of them are now proprietors or part owners of English refineries.

To the Germans, no doubt, Britain is indebted for the art of refining sugar: but chiefly to her own citizens is she indebted for any improvements that have been introduced in connection with the refining process. The Germans, to speak of them generally, possess many good and amiable qualities: they are for the most part ingenious, industrious and intelligent. But this opinion must be somewhat modified in speaking of that class of them connected with the process of sugar refining in this country, who, with but few exceptions, have proved themselves to be rather illiterate, selfish, and indeed treacherous towards our countrymen, as we shall probably have occasion to show. They, too, in many cases, it must be admitted, assumed a position in our refineries which, in fact, they were quite unjustified in occupying. They pretended (from prejudice no doubt) that it was an absolute impossibility for those of this country to become practical sugar refiners, or even to attain to anything like a comprehensive

or practical view of the refining process. They likewise held, on the other hand, that their countrymen or those in any way connected by blood-relationship to Germans (who, it may be, had never previously seen a sugarhouse) were quite competent to conduct the whole sugar refining process in the various departments. Their success in imposing upon the refiners of this country may be inferred from the exorbitant salaries and perquisites they received under the guise of such pretensions, and, perhaps, more so, from the honour and respect, or rather the homage and reverence, claimed by and paid to those foreigners alike on the part of master and workmen.

… The Germans, so to speak, kept the "proofstick" a sealed book; and to all others than Germans or their descendants it remained so. They, in short, locked up the door to the knowledge of the sugar refining trade in this country, taking with them the key: they entered not in themselves (in so far as improvements in the refining process were concerned), and those of our countrymen that were entering in, they hindered.

It is unfortunate that Robert Niccol offered so little support for his very one-sided opinions. Whether these were his own findings based upon personal experience, or the pickings from his visits to refineries and/or conversations with refinery owners and workers, we may never know. He did write well on the technical aspects of the industry in the mid-1800s, so maybe his attack was based on at least some first-hand knowledge. John M Hutcheson,[43] in 1901, simply commented objectively – *"Many of these foreigners were excellent men, but for something like 50 years prior to 1850 most of them were autocrats of unquestionable sternness."* (It would appear that both men were born in Greenock in 1832 and were living in Union Street at the time of the 1881 census, which shows Niccol as unmarried and a "Practical Sugar Refiner & Author Unemployed" and Hutcheson as married and a "Sugar Broker". The former published his work aged 32, the latter aged 69!)

The naturalisation memorials of 1851 for Lear Wrede of Greenock rather support the

Hutcheson view – "[Mr Wrede is] personally known to us to be a person of credit and respectability and of undoubted loyalty..." and "... Mr Wrede is most exemplary in all the relations of life... and he is much and deservedly respected in the town, by all who have the pleasure of knowing him".[44]

Just what did the refinery owners and managers, the Germans in particular, do for their men and their communities? We know that the owners of the larger refineries, mainly in London, provided accommodation for their single migrant workers, and if Hall & Boyd in Breezers Hill in 1836 was anything to go by, this was no mean provision but a series of rooms on three floors with kitchen and beer cellar.[45] Whilst this did give them control over the men, it also provided support for the new arrivals by placing them within a culture and language with which they were familiar.

There are hundreds of sugar refiners' wills available to us, many showing considerable generosity, but one may possibly be unique – that of Johann George Wicke proved in 1829. With a sugarhouse in Church Lane, Whitechapel, and a home in Stratford Green, Essex, he was a very wealthy man. He not only left legacies of £100 to each of his boilers and £100 to each clerk with £150 to his chief clerk, which was not unusual for the time, but also £12 to each of his labourers who had worked for him for 2 years or more and £6 to each of those who had worked for less than 2 years. This was probably the act of a truly considerate man, for he also instructed that on his death his sugarhouse was to be sold, possibly leaving his employees without work.[46]

John Wagener, originally from Trendelburg, Hessen, and with a refinery in Mansel Street, built a row of houses off Gower's Walk which, according to the censuses of 1851 and 1861, were occupied in part by sugarbakers. Wagener was one of those refiners who became wealthy enough to move out of the East End to Essex, purchasing Gt Langtons, a large mansion in Hornchurch where, even after his death, his family continued their charitable works in the local area.[47]

St Paul's German Reformed Church (established in 1697 at the chapel of the Savoy Palace; consecrated in Hooper Square in 1819; moved to Goulston Street in the 1880s) and St George's German Lutheran Church (founded in Alie Street in 1763) served the German communities in the East End of London.[48] The latter, which also had a school, had been founded by the wealthy sugarbaker, Dederich Beckmann, and became the place of worship of many German sugarbakers, rich and poor alike. As the rich got richer they moved out of the confines of St George's in the East and Whitechapel to the villages of Essex, Middlesex and Surrey prompting the church to arrange services during the weekday afternoons whilst the refiners were "in town" to oversee their businesses, rather than risk losing their wealthy benefactors. Both churches received money from subscribers, as well as legacies in wills, to provide care and education within their communities. Some of those from sugar refiners are listed below[49]:

St George's...

1773	Deichmann, G	£100
1789	Wittick, G	£100
1792	Samler, H	£200
1803	Briebach, M	£2
1806	Bott, Joh	£100
1809	Detmar, Jos	£200
1809	Knies, Andr	£100
1822	Dettmar, J	£180
1824	Harbusch, JH	£100
1828	Muhm, H	£500
1829	Wicke, G	£300
1834	Harbusch, Werner	£500
1842	Mogge, H	£10

St George's School...

1829	Wicke, G	£100
1834	Harbusch, Werner	£500

St Paul's...

1812	Dirs, CH	£50
1823	Lilckendey, G	£20
1826	Witte, Ludw	£100
1829	Wicke, Georg	£100
1833	Ringen, C	£77
1834	Harbusch, Werner	£100
1842	Garms, L	£25

1843	Bischoff, Joh	£48

Charity did not just stay within the German community, for other groups benefited from the generosity of the refiners. In 1801 an Agreement of Subsidies for Maintenance of Roads[50] included G Wackerbarth, Thomas Hodgson, Walton & Witte, Henry Eggars and Matthew Craven, and in 1820 the Committee of the East London Irish Free School[51] in Goodman's Yard reported the following subscribers, among others, known to be in the sugar industry…

- Burnell, J of Whitechapel Road
- Carlill, J of Leman Street
- Coope, J of Osborn Street
- Friend, E & Co of Charlotte Street
- Harbusch, W of Commercial Road
- Holthouse & Detmar of Back Lane
- Hodgeson & Son of Goodmans Stile
- Lucas & Son of Osborne Street
- Lucas & Martin of Back Lane
- Martineau, P & Son of Goulston Square
- Martineau, J & Son of Leman Street
- Mum, H of Whitechapel Road
- Schroder, J & Son of Princes Pl
- Schlinker, G of Dock Street
- Wagentrieber, JC of Whitechapel Road
- Witte & Buck of Well Street
- Walton, Fairbank & Co of Lambeth Street
- Vulliamy, L of Edmonton

Court Henry Dirs of Wellclose Square, in his will of 1812 left £300 to "the Middlesex Society for educating Poor Children in Protestant religion" in Cannon Street Road,[52] and numerous other wills show charitable legacies to the poor and the education of the young. The London Hospital in Whitechapel Road benefited from donations particularly at the time of serious sugarhouse accidents and fires, when owners and workers alike would collect for both the treatment of the injured and the care of the grieving families. As general concern grew in London in the 1840s over the social conditions, the German Hospital was founded at Dalston; the Deutche Wohltätigkeitsgesellschaft, a mutual-aid association, extended its activities to the East End; and the Deutsche Evangelische

Stadtmission in London was formed by German Protestant congregations to work among the East End poor.[53] In 1851, of the 398 male in-patients at the German Hospital, 127 were sugarbakers.[54]

Just like the benefactors of, and subscribers to, these charitable works, the beneficiaries were also from assorted faiths and backgrounds. The following examples are taken from the Accounts of the Society of Friends of Foreigners in Distress, London, 1838 and 1853[55]:

– Bort, George, 16 West Street, Mile End, aged 73, a native of Wurtemburg, 53 years in England. After having worked in various sugar-houses he set up for himself and carried on business very successfully, as he states, but failed at last in consequence of misplaced confidence. Since then he endeavoured, by hard work, as long as he was able, to gain his livelihood but is now (as well as his wife who is older than himself) totally unfit for labour. Their only son who behaved in a most exemplary manner to his parents died, about a year ago, and they have now nothing to depend on but the scanty pittance which two unnmarried daughters earn by their needle-work, and a trifling allowance from another quarter.

– Stock, Daniel Frederick, 1 Eastfield Street, Stepney, aged 81, a native of Glenhausen [Gelnhausen?], near Frankfurt, fifty-two years in this country. By trade he was a sugar-baker, having been in the employ of one master for eight years and of another for twenty; is severely ruptured and afflicted with rheumatism, which quite disables him for work. He latterly obtained a scanty livelihood by vending sweetmeats, but his bodily infirmities are such as to prevent him any longer earning a subsistence by this means. He has been kept from absolute starvation through the kindness of relatives whose means are very limited. His only other resource is an allowance of 2s. per week from this Society.

– Von Zalzen, Johann, 21 Cudworth Street, North Street, Mile End, aged 76, a native of Hanover, fifty-one years in this country. He

maintained himself and family creditably for upwards of thirty years as a sugar-baker, and when his strength failed him, he did what he could to get a living wherever he could find employment; but he is quite past labour, being in ill health and very infirm. His wife, an Englishwoman, seventy years of age, earns a trifle by washing and shoe-binding, but she is likewise in declining health, and this industrious and aged couple are now reduced to a miserable state of distress. The parish refuse to assist them unless they go into the workhouse, and an allowance of 2s. per week from this Society is consequently their only present source of relief.

Herman Schriever died in 1897, and in the year prior to his death had just the 3s per week from the Society of Friends of Foreigners in Distress to depend upon.[56] He appears to have worked at Martineau's at 6 Christian Street for over 30 years; however, the 1891 census points to its imminent closure with only himself and a few other sugarbakers listed in the neighbourhood including Ahrens, Otterstedt, Dreyer, Marcks and Meyer. Martineau's was almost the last of the East End refineries, David Martineau having already purchased James Duncan's refinery in Silvertown in 1887 and become a neighbour of Abram Lyle and Henry Tate.

The Glaswegian, James Duncan, participated in the efforts to improve the poor living conditions in the area, and paid a doctor £300 a year to attend his men. He built two churches, one Congregational and one Presbyterian with their own schoolrooms, and made considerable donations to projects of other faiths. He would pay for a day at the seaside for his employees and families, some 3000 in number. Henry Tate, a Unitarian from Liverpool and, of course, famous for the Tate Gallery on Millbank, was responsible for much more both in London and in other parts of the country. Liverpool's university and homeopathic hospital, and colleges in Oxford and London, benefited from major donations. The Plaistow area benefited much from the Lyle family from Greenock, in particular Queen Mary's Hospital at Stratford.[57]

The "expert strangers" had come to the UK, some 350 years earlier, to introduce the process of refining sugar to a new market. They would earn good money, and would be instrumental in developing a need for this new product, thus increasing production and earnings. Nothing much had changed then, for innovators and businessmen still had the same objectives and, just like today, employers aimed for the best production from the best workers they could afford to employ. Their reign had ended, however, for with London's sugarhouses all but closed, new regimes had taken over on the Essex marshes at Silvertown, and German names amongst the workforce were few. A photograph taken in 1881 at Tate's Thames Refinery, contained only 3 names out of some 44 that might be identified with German sugarbakers.[58] An early photograph of Lyle's workforce at Plaistow Wharf in 1892 contains just one who would have worked with sugar and two others, a cooper and a case maker, out of 83.[59]

Niccol had got his way. The Scots had taken over, recruited from both Greenock and Liverpool for these new refineries – the best men for the job in the eyes of Lyle and Tate (who would not become Tate & Lyle for many years yet). In 1965 a record of the activities of the Tate & Lyle Group would read, *"The Scots names are still ringing round the public address system at Plaistow. The name of Lyle is one of them. But Charles Mackay, foreman blacksmith, had eleven children working in the refinery. Two generations of Mackays, three generations of McGlones, four generations of McMarths and five generations of Lyles have worked in Plaistow".*[60]

The one thing Robert Niccol was probably right about was that the Germans looked after their own – quite natural for any migrant group in a new country.

Curt Muhm was born in 1653 in Gleichen, Hessen, and had a grandson, Jost Heinrich, born in 1746 who came to London and set himself up in the sugar refining business. He soon anglicised his name to Henry Mum, and the earliest note of him is in 1789 in Alie Street, Whitechapel.[61] He worked in this area until his death in about 1827, at one time in partnership with John Craven, and probably also with his nephew, Henry Martin. The majority of Henry Mum's estate went to his great nephew Michael Muhm, born 1802 in Schwabendorf, Hessen. Michael had recently arrived in London from Germany to work in the same trade as Henry and benefit from his great-uncle's experience and wealth.

Michael Muhm worked in Gloucester Street, Mile End, but for much of his life he lived in Shadwell. Michael had nine children, two of whom followed his trade. Frederick Muhm is noted in 1865 in partnership with Muller in Gower's Walk,[62] whilst Stratford Muhm is listed in the 1901 census aged 52, lunatic and retired sugar boiler, a patient at Bethnal House, Bethnal Green.

In his will[63] Henry Mum left a total of £12,000 to his nieces and nephews back in Germany and asked that £6,900 plus the proceeds from the sale of various items be given in specified amounts to the British and Foreign Bible Society, the Missionary Society, the Countess of Huntingdon's College, the Zion Chapel in Union Street, the Middlesex Society for the Educating of Poor Children in the Protestant Religion, Tower Hamlets Charity School, the Whitechapel Society for the Education of the Poor and the New German Chapel in Rupert Street. He also gave considerable financial assistance to the family of the late Herman Almeroth, probably having cared for them for 15 years since the untimely death at 50 of their husband and father. Herman Almeroth, *"a sugar loaf maker from Saxony"*,[64] was my four times great-grandfather, and I am convinced he worked for Henry Mum for many years, with Henry taking him under his wing until he was experienced enough to set up his own small sugarhouse for the 3 or 4 years prior to his death in 1812.

Notes

1 The National Archives – BT 31/14384/3063.
2 *The Plaistow Story* by Oliver Lyle, Tate & Lyle, 1960 (with names).
3 *Sugar & All That: a History of Tate & Lyle* by Antony Hugill, Gentry Books 1978 (without names).
4 Hugill (note 3).
5 London Metropolitan Archives – E/MW/C/229.
6 *The History of Sugar* by Noel Deerr, Chapman & Hall, 1950.
7 Glasgow Commisary Court Wills.
8 Bristol Record Office – 36772 Box 3.
9 Deerr (note 6).
10 *Bloody Foreigners* by Robert Winder, Abacus, 2005.
11 Parish Registers of St Martin in the Fields, Westminster, London.
12 The National Archives PROB 11/862.
13 Cliff Webb Apprentices Lists.
14 The National Archives C104/211.
15 (see note 14).
16 (see note 14).
17 *Notes on the Sugar Industry of the United Kingdom* by John M Hutcheson, James McKelvie, 1901.
18 Webb (note 13).
19 Guildhall Library – Sun Fire Office Insurance Policies.
20 Northamptonshire Record Office BrW221.
21 Sun (note 19).
22 *Things Phoenix 1782–1982* by K B Croker, Penshurst Press, 1982.
23 The National Archives PROB11/1222.
24 The National Archives HO4.
25 The National Archives HO1/36/1261 XC/A/11301.
26 Northamptonshire Record Office HOLT 404.
27 Northamptonshire Record Office HOLT 268–272.
28 Society of Genealogists Lists of Bankrupts.
29 Northamptonshire Record Office HOLT 622. (The Holthouse of Hellidon collection was gifted to the Northamptonshire Record Office with the main accessions being in 1937 and 1950. Whilst they have given permission in respect of any owner's right in the collection, they request that I state that their best endeavours have been made to trace copyright owners, and information is welcomed where this has not been established.)
30 1) Censuses. 2) Len Metzner's Shipping Lists from The National Archives HO2 & HO3.
31 *Die Zuckerbacker waren vornehmlich Hannoveraner* by Horst Rössler, 2003.
32 *Germans in the British Sugar Industry: Work, Culture, Religion*, Horst Rössler, lecture at Greenwich, July 2004.

33 *The Settlement of Germans in Britain during the Nineteenth Century* by Panikos Panayi, IMIS – Beiträge, Heft 14, June 2000.

34 Whitaker's Almanack, 1998, The Stationery Office.

35 Panayi (note 32).

36 *A Hundred Years of Sugar Refining – the story of Love Lane Refinery 1872–1972* by J A Watson, Tate & Lyle, 1973.

37 IGI submission.

38 Baines Lancashire Directory.

39 Gore's Liverpool Directory.

40 *The Failure of Utah's First Sugar Factory*, by Charles L Schmalz, Utah Historical Quarterly, 1988, vol 56, no 1.

41 Wilson's Dublin Directory 1760.

42 "Essay on Sugar, and general treatise on sugar refining, as practised in the Clyde Refineries: Embracing the Latest Improvements" by Robert Niccol: Practical Sugar Refiner, Greenock. Printed by A. Mackenzie & Co, 1864.

43 Hutcheson (note 17).

44 The National Archives HO1/36/1261 XC/A/11301.

45 Tower Hamlets Local History Library – Deeds TH4174 .

46 The National Archives PROB 11/1756.

47 *Essex and Sugar* by Frank Lewis, Phillimore & Co Ltd, 1976.

48 Registers deposited at Tower Hamlets Local History Library. Abstracts on fiche available from AGFHS.

49 *Geschichte der deutschen evangelischen Kirchen in England*, by Carl Schoell, London/Stuttgart 1852.

50 Tower Hamlets Local History Library.

51 Tower Hamlets Local History Library – LP4011.

52 Will Oxford 216 July 1812.

53 "The German Factor in London History" by Patricia Hawes, AGFHS Mitteilungsblatt Extra Editon 1988.

54 Schoell (note 47).

55 Accounts of the Society of Friends of Foreigners in Distress, (Established 1806), for Years 1838 & 1853, London: Schulze & Co.

56 Society of Friends (note 53).

57 Lewis (note 45).

58 Tate photo (note 3).

59 Lyle photo (note 2).

60 *Tate & Lyle – a record of the activities of The Tate & Lyle Group, 1965*, Tate & Lyle.

61 Andrews Directory 1789.

62 Post Office Directory 1868.

63 The National Archives PROB 11/1739.

64 Family lore.

THE BOX

From a pamphlet describing a N Buckinghamshire town, early 20C…

"The trotting of horses in those days was a far more pleasing sign than the present motor car or motor cycle with its poisonous fumes. What a common sight it was to see a box of a well known sugar firm, mounted on wheels, pushed along the streets with the necessary shovel to pick up the manure and deposit same on the garden."

Through the Centuries in Olney and District, by Sidney F Morgan

Where did they live and work?

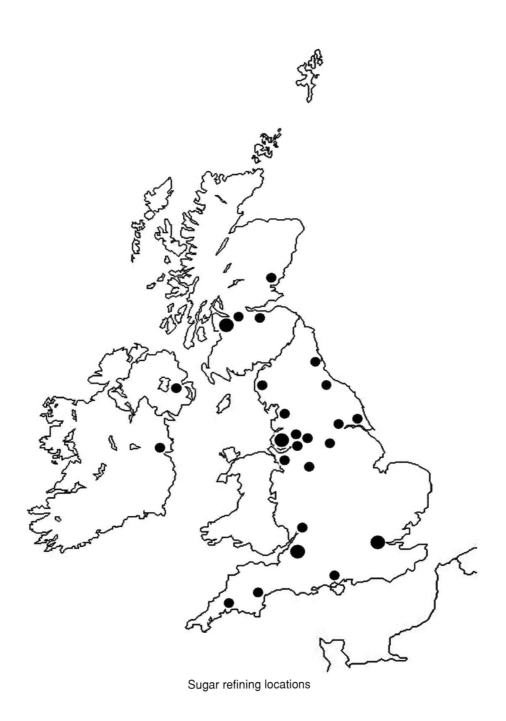

Sugar refining locations

The marriage of Herman Almeroth and Sarah Bass took place in 1793 at St Dunstan, Stepney. The baptism entries of their children over the next 10 years show they lived in Half Moon Alley, Whitechapel High Street and Duncan Street, all in the tiny area of Whitechapel just above Alie Street. Henry Mum's sugarhouse was in Duncan Street throughout this period, so if this was indeed where Herman worked, he would have had only a few yards to walk to work.

This appears to have been typical. Those who did not live at the refinery usually lived very close. Hours were very long, starts very early, and too much walking time was avoided. Whilst locating where people lived before the 1841 census is limited to parish registers, of which only some include such information, and occasionally other documents, our tasks were made easier once the censuses began recording addresses. If you scroll through the census entries for St George's in the East it's easy to see that labourers lived with their families either in the street in which the sugarhouse was located or an adjoining street. Few walked more than two streets to work. In general, this pattern was repeated throughout the refining towns and cities.

Those workers newly recruited from Germany, and those who remained single, were often housed in the *Men's Rooms* provided on site by the refinery owners. This not only gave them greater control over their employees but also gave them labour on hand 24 hours a day. Fires and boilers needed lighting in the early hours of the morning. This refinery-provided accommodation varied considerably from purpose built rooms to "the house next door", and it was usual for the master boiler who was in charge of the men during work time to live either in the Men's Rooms with his own family or in an attached dwelling house. The refinery of Hall & Boyd in Breezers Hill, St George's in the East, had its own Men's Rooms, and the deeds[1] for its transfer to John Hall and James Boyd in 1833 and 1836 tell us this was a 3-storey building with two rooms on each floor and a beer cellar beneath. The parlour and kitchen on the ground floor and

the 4 upper rooms had plastered walls and stone hearths, and all rooms had doors with locks and bolts. The 1841 census shows 23 men living here, in 1851 it was 21 and in 1861 there were 32 – and all of these were German. At Martineau's, 6 Christian Street, there appear to have been 22 men living-in in 1851, 53 in 1861 and 34 in 1871. In 1851 Friend and Boden at 17 Fieldgate Street utilised the house next door, possibly a public house, as Men's Rooms. Fifteen men lived there, all but one German, whilst William Boden lived in the dwelling house at the refinery. By 1861, No 16 Fieldgate Street was certainly "The Kings Arms" with publican John Gerken living there with his family and 8 German sugarbakers as lodgers. In 1871 only Richard Phillips and William Emis, the gatekeeper, were at No 17, and the pub had closed, although more than 30 ordinary folks were living at the address. However, when the large refinery was advertised for sale in 1882 following the death of Mr Hodge, the owner, some 6 years earlier, the *"freehold dwelling house No 16 Fieldgate Street containing 12 rooms and in the basement a mess room for the men"* was included in the sale.[2] A sample from the 1851 census shows 17 men at Peter Martineau's in Goulston Street, 37 men at Craven & Lucas in Leman Street, 34 men at Fred Bowman's in Alie Street, 40 men at Elers & Morgan in Lambeth Street and 50 men at Goodhart's in Horseferry Road, Limehouse. This appears to have been very much a London thing and very much a German thing: such Men's Rooms do not appear to have existed in the other refining centres, at least during census time.

Those men who lived-out, whether married, in homes with their families, or single, in lodgings, would have had to pay rent to either a local landlord or to the head of the family who had sub-let their rooms. Multiple-occupancy was very common indeed, with either two or three families in one house or one family with any number of lodgers. It is likely this was the only way some families could afford the rent. The censuses show that sugarbakers very often had other sugarbakers of the same nationality lodging with them, and this undoubtedly gave a sense of community whether it was the Germans in Whitechapel or the Irish in Greenock.

As London's East End sugarhouses were mostly built early in the 19th century, the housing around them was of a similar period or earlier. Whilst Whitechapel was dotted with substantial Georgian dwellings, shops and inns, it was not in these that the workers lived. They dwelt in the maze of alleys and yards behind them that Millicent Rose[3] describes as "shanties of wood and plaster that made up the back-alley rookeries", and in the terraces hurriedly built on the small meadows and market gardens to the south and east of St Mary's Church.

Liverpool and Greenock had more space, and their new refineries were built later with housing added to keep pace with expansion. Nevertheless, they still did not necessarily get it right. In Ann Street, Greenock, close to the Clyde Refinery on Drumfrochar Road, terraces of large tenement-type dwellings were built, each housing over a dozen families – the 1881 census shows around 40 sugarhouse labourers, almost all Irish, living in those closest to the refinery. Liverpool concentrated on cramming as many families as possible into the space available, even though there was plenty of new land to build on. The new refineries of Macfie, Fairrie, Leitch, Crossfield, Tate and Jager were all built north of the city centre, but when the opportunities arose to improve the type and quality of new housing they were not taken. Not having learnt from the mistakes of the 18th century, new courts and cramped terraces were built, and new slums were added to old.

* * *

Perhaps we should take a closer look at where the sugarbakers worked, and maybe where they lived, in each of the refining towns and cities. Clear sketch maps for each city or town, showing approximate locations of refineries and the names of those who ran them, are available on the Sugar Refiners and Sugarbakers website at www.mawer.clara.net.

Bristol…

In the middle of the street, as far as you can see, hundreds of ships, their masts as thick as they can stand by one another, which is the oddest and most surprising sight imaginable… a long street full of ships in the middle and houses on both sides looks like a dream. – Alexander Pope, 1739[4]

Quite a different Bristol from that of today. You probably stand in a similar place to where Pope stood when you wait for the bus to the Record Office, but his ships have been replaced by buses and cars, the smell of tar and sugar by exhaust fumes, and the shouts of sailors and merchants by traffic noise. We have to remember that at this time both the River Avon and the River Frome ran through the centre of Bristol, for they were the arteries of a city which had become the main British port for transatlantic trade. The Frome came into the city from the north east, crossed Penn Street and roughly followed the line of Fairfax Street, Silver Street and Rupert Street, before running down between St Augustine's Parade and Broad Quay to join the Avon. The Avon, of course, was tidal, leaving ships lying on mud banks at low tide. It was not until the Floating Harbour, a non-tidal basin where the two rivers met, was created (1804–9) that ships could float upright and be loaded and unloaded at all states of the tide.[5]

Arguably, Bristol's two most important sugarhouses were those at St Peter's and Counterslip, the first and almost the last, the smallest and the largest. In 1612, Robert Aldworth converted part of Norton's House, next to the churchyard of St Peter's, into a one-pan sugarhouse, and it was the city's only sugarhouse until 1654. With gardens sloping down to the Avon providing the access to shipments of raw sugar, the house continued a small but growing trade under various owners – Aldworth sold to Giles Elbridge, who sold to Robert and Thomas Challoner,[6] who sold to Richard Beauchampe. The inventory taken for this last sale in 1666 showed total stocks of refined sugars, syrups and molasses in excess of 72 tons and stocks of raw sugar of just over 4 tons, with a total value of about £2600.[7] By the time Conrad Finzel took over the Counterslip refinery in 1839 it had been running under various ownership for a century and a half. His initial efforts were destroyed by fire in 1846, but this gave him the opportunity to totally rebuild and create the country's largest refinery to date. Finzel died in 1859 and his son, also Conrad, took over. This was a huge building across the Avon from the site of the old St Peter's sugarhouse. Highly mechanized with the very latest vacuum pans and centrifugal machines, it is said to have produced over 1200 tons of sugar a week and employed over 700 workers at its peak. The decline in the Bristol sugar trade saw it close, however, in 1881.[8]

St John's Bridge Sugar House / Hotel du Vin, Bristol, © Bryan Mawer

In between were numerous sugar refining concerns. Bristol was known for its sugar refining families such as Knight, Pope, Garlick, Daubeny and Brice; for its heavy involvement in the slave trade; for its unique insistence, at least in the early years, upon an apprenticeship with a grocer being a pre-requisite for entry into the refining trade; and its strong connections with the Non-Conformist churches, of which a number of refiners were major benefactors.

The second sugarhouse was set up in St Augustine's Back in 1653 by John Knight, and was considerably larger than the first as well as having thirteen new cottages built in its grounds for the workers.[9] The most important of the 18th century must be the St John's Bridge sugarhouse on Lewins Mead facing St John's Bridge, which then crossed the River Frome immediately outside the front door of the sugarhouse. Built in 1728 by Edward Reed, a member of the Unitarian Meeting House next door, this was simply yet another Bristol sugarhouse... but it is extremely important because it is still standing!

The sugarhouse closed in 1834 and after various uses lay empty for some years before being carefully converted into the Hotel du Vin in 1999. So when next in Lewins Mead take a look at the hotel with new eyes, for the main building is almost 300 years old with the buildings to the rear added later to house the boilers and steam engine. Read the board at the entrance relating the building's varied history.

Bristol had a large number of sugarhouses in a small area. The published and unpublished research of the late Mr I V Hall[10] and the more recent little book by Donald Jones[11] are the chief sources of information regarding the industry in Bristol. The city refined sugar for exactly 300 years, with the research showing evidence of refineries in...

- 1612–1696   St Peter's Sugar House
- 1653–1708   St Augustine's Back
- 1661–1783   St Thomas Street
- 1662–1784   Temple Street
- 1665–1824   Whitson Court
- 1681–1881   Counterslip
- 1684–1826   Lewins Mead (2 houses)
- 1684–1912   Old Market
- 1685–1790   Tucker Street
- 1689–1816   Redcliffe Street (2 houses)
- 1712–1817   Halliers Lane/Bridewell Lane
- 1715–1763   Duck Lane
- 1724–1812   Old King Street
- 1728–1834   St John's Bridge

- 1750–1815   Great George Street/Traitors Bridge
- 1754–1849   Wilder Street
- 1760–1830   Nelson Street
- 1760–1859   Quay Head
- 1775–1809   Temple Back
- 1777–1840   Quakers Friars
- 1787–1840   Host Street
- 1797–1808   Guinea Street
- 1867–1906   Castle Street

…as well as Red Lodge Street, Upper Maudlin Lane, Small Street, St Stephen Street, Merchant Street, Cathay, Back Street, Blackfriars and at Bristol Bridge.

Chester…

For some 160 years sugar was refined in Chester, though on quite a small scale and probably for local consumption. Giles Vanbrugh, the father of Sir John, and Anthony, John and Samuel Henthorne refined in Chester in the late 17th century, and there was a sugar house in Weavers Lane in 1745, which in the 1780s was run by Robert Hesketh and John Kennerly. Also in the 1780s there was a sugarhouse in Skinners Lane on the banks of the River Dee, probably run by Thomas Roberts. There is little known of these businesses, but considerable information is to be found at the Record Office in Chester regarding the rather short-lived sugarhouse in Cuppins Lane.[12]

On the south side of Cuppins Lane once stood five cottages that by 1740 had been demolished and the land, after various uses, was sold in 1752/3 to Benjamin Wilson, a sugarbaker from Liverpool. The building of a three pan sugar house in Cuppins Lane was probably begun in early 1755, but whether Wilson began the sugarhouse by himself is not known. In 1756 he and his wife made an agreement with John Hincks of Chester and Joseph Manesty of Liverpool for the running of the business. Wilson was the refiner working the sugar house, Manesty in Liverpool was purchasing the raw sugar, and Hincks, a merchant and later referred to as banker, appears to have been brokering

business for the concern. The partnership does not appear to have got off to a good start, for by the beginning of 1758 questions were being asked by Hincks about Manesty's methods of buying sugar. In March a large bill for 55 hogsheads of raw sugar valued at £1343. 9s. 8$\frac{1}{2}$d was presented by Francis Perkins of Liverpool. Wilson accused Manesty of paying too high a price for sugar, and Manesty complained that there was no money available to pay the "Excise Man" for an earlier 50-hogshead order. In the same year a document was drawn up dissolving the partnership! It's doubtful that the partnership was ever dissolved, perhaps they all had too much invested and too much to lose, for in 1764 the business was still running with the same partners and the same shares. Joseph Manesty wished to be released from the partnership, however, and by the end of that same year bankruptcy had been filed against him by his creditors in Liverpool.

Benjamin Wilson died in the mid-1760s, and Hincks in 1772, although probate of his will was not granted for some 5 or 6 years, by which time the business was in a bad way. Robert Hincks, John's brother, who had been running the sugarhouse, walked out after a dispute regarding unpaid debts to Wilson's estate, leaving Arbella Hincks, John's widow, with a failing business. She did not take the advice of Samuel Norcott, a Manchester refiner, to close the business, instead investing further along with another partner, William Boult. She appears to have managed to clear her debts, but there is little further evidence of the sugarhouse. The Hunter map of 1789 shows sugarhouses in Weavers Lane and Skinners Lane, but not the one in Cuppins Lane, and the directories of that year and the years to follow make no mention of it.

Dublin…

Dublin's first sugarhouse was run by John and Peter Paumier, from Bordeaux, at Mullinahack, near Cook Street, from about 1745. Within a few years more had sprung up in the area around the castle and close to either side of the River Liffey. Hawkins Street,

George's Street, Stephen Street, Fade Street, Francis Street, Henry Street, Skinner's Alley and Aston Quay all had sugarhouses by 1760, and Mary's Lane, Mary's Abbey, Abbey Street and Exchequer Street by 1780.[13] As the city grew, newer refineries were built just a little further from the centre. John Jaggers, in partnership with others, had three refineries by 1846 in Princes Street South, Gloucester Street South and Earl Street South. John O'Flaherty was at 166 King Street North a few years later, though not for too long as Robert Blair, a Greenock refiner, is said to have run Dublin's only refinery from 1881–6.[14]

Earlestown...

The Sankey Sugar Works at Earlestown is rather a special case. Begun in 1855, situated on the main Liverpool and Manchester Railway and the St Helens Canal, and on the edge of Newton-in-Makerfield, it was isolated from other refineries. We can be sure, therefore, that the sugar workers included in the local censuses were working there, rather than at any one of a number of refineries as in most other towns and cities. The refinery was built against the canal with railway lines coming right to the door, and it also had its own reservoirs. Most importantly, the triangular site bounded by the railway, canal and woodland, was laid out to accommodate many of those who worked there.

From the 1891 map and the 1861–1901 censuses we can work out that Sankey Hill House was the owner's house and there were two smaller detached houses, Larkfield and Higher Astley, used variously by the sons of the owner, and the clerk to the Works, Thomas Haselden. Close to the refinery buildings were two rows of dwellings – nos 1–10 were a terrace of small cottages allocated to the assistant boilers, Thomas Tunstall, William Goodwin and Thomas Pill, and some of the labourers. Nos 11–16 were three pairs of larger semi-detached cottages, 11/12 built before 1881, 13/14 between 1881 and 1891, and 15/16 between 1891 and 1906. Claus Heinrich Schuhmacher, from Hanover, was foreman boiler and lived at no 11, with James Wrigley,

a mechanic, at no 12. A couple of hundred yards from the Works were cottages built for the labourers in the form of three long terraces each of about a dozen houses around three sides of the wonderfully named Vitriol Square. By 1901 these appear to have been renamed Shop Row, London Row and Engineers Row.

In 1861 more than 50 workers lived on site, many with their families, but they were listed only as being at the "Sugar Works", and few lived in the nearby town. Disappointingly, in 1871 the enumerators simply used the word "labourer", and failed to distinguish between the different workplaces and trades in the area. From 1881 to 1901 the number of workers living in Newton-in-Makerfield gradually increased, probably indicating both a larger workforce and a move towards the better amenities of the expanding town. In 1935 the Works was taken over by Manbré & Garton.

Edinburgh and Leith...

Canongate Sugar House, at 160 Canongate, was run by Francis Kamptie in the 1770s–80s[15] and later by Wm Macfie & Co. Macfie was refining out by Leith Docks, in Elbe Street, 1804–35, and at Canongate 1829–52.[16] Also in Leith were the Leith Sugar Refining Co in Coburg Street to about 1852 and the Bonnington Sugar Refining Co in Breadalbane Street 1866–80.[17] There is earlier evidence though of the trade in the area – George Simpson is listed as a workman in a sugarhouse in Leith at his marriage in 1763 at South Leith Kirk, whilst Robert Fraser was married in 1753 as was Peter Soat in 1769, both at the Old Kirk, Edinburgh, and both sugarhouse workers. There is a 1752 directory entry for St Christopher's Sugar House in North Foulis Close, off the High Street.[18]

Glasgow...

This is where Scotland's sugar was produced in the early years, with two sugarhouses in the 1660s and four more built before refining began so successfully along the Clyde in

Greenock. The Western Sugar House (1667–1787) in Candlerigg Street and the Eastern Sugar House (1669–1799) in Gallowgate were the first. The latter is where Zacharius Zebbes was boiler, and as well as the detailed information regarding the personnel that springs from his will, there is also a painting of the actual sugarhouse available to us, albeit from the mid-1800s when in a rather dilapidated state.[19] It was No 138 Gallowgate, situated in Sugar House Close between Gallowgate and London Street, with narrow lanes and rows of buildings close down each side. A solid rectangular building of yellow stone, it stood 5 storeys high and probably had cellars beneath and garrets in its double-pitched roof.

In the first half of the 18th century, the Little Sugar House was built in King Street along with the King Street Sugar House, also the South Sugar House in Stockwell Street. The North Sugar House was built almost next door to the Western Sugar House in Bell's Wynd soon after. Most of these houses were run by partnerships of businessmen, with the initial management of the Western Sugar House involving 10 men.

The 19th century brought sugarhouses in Queen Street, Washington Street, High John Street, Alston Street (where the present Central Railway Station now stands) and Oswald Street. All the refineries were close to the centre of the city and close to the River Clyde. Just the one was built out at Port Dundas on the Forth and Clyde Canal and this, along with Washington Street, was probably the last to close around 1877.[20]

Greenock…

This is the easy one – John Hutcheson[21] in his excellent book of 1901 meticulously listed all the refineries chronologically with their histories, whilst R M Smith[22] gave us further information in 1921 – and so to summarize…

1. Sugar House Lane (at foot of) – Greenock Sugar House Co – built in 1765 by 7 merchants who took on Mark Kuhll as boiler in return for a one-eighth share in the business. Various owners including Harm Blanken and James Fairrie, before Robert Kerr made it Brewers Sugar Co from 1885 to 1921.

2. Sugar House Lane (at south of) – built by a partnership that included Robert Macfie, and employed Nicolus Witt as boiler, in 1788. It was eventually run as Alexander Currie & Co until 1886, before being converted into lodging houses.

3. Bogle Street – Robert Macfie & Sons built this one in 1802 and operated there until 1854, before moving to Liverpool.

4. Cartsdyke Bridge – James Fairrie & Co, established in 1809, burned down in 1846. Of the Fairrie brothers who took over the business when their father, James, died in 1815, Thomas continued in Greenock, John in London and Adam in Liverpool, but always as a family partnership.

5. Clarence Street – Glebe Sugar House – 1812–1847, destroyed by fire.

6. Princes Street – Princes Street Works – began in 1826. Purchased by John Walker & Co in 1848, burned down 3 times but still operating well into 20th century.

7. Shaws Water – 1829. Lear Wrede refined here for a few years before 1851. Destroyed by fire in 1864, rebuilt and worked until about 1883.

8. Ker Street – Greenock Sugar Refinery, later Glebe Sugar Refining Co. Built on part of the site of the original Glebe Sugar House (5) in 1831, Fairrie took it over in 1845, but importantly this was the refinery of Abram Lyle along with partners Kerr, Grieve and Hunter, from 1865. Lyle retired in 1882 to set up in London, but the company was continued by the Kerr and Grieve families into the next century.

9. Baker Street (at foot of) – 1831, burned down in 1851.

10. Roxburgh Street – built in 1832, pulled down and rebuilt in 1874, eventually wound up in 1896.

11. Port Glasgow Road – Cappielow Refinery – built by Speirs & Wrede in 1833, destroyed by fire in 1841, rebuilt by Speirs and worked until 1859. Bought by A Anderson and Sons, fires again in both

1872 and 1877 after which it was not rebuilt.

12. Inverkip Street (south end) – 1847–1857, destroyed by fire. Part of the site became Greenock West Station.

13. Main Street, Cartsdyke – 1847–1848, destroyed by fire.

14. Ingleston Street – Blair, Reid & Steele in 1847. After 2 fires, it was run by Robert Blair alone towards the end of its life, and wound up in 1881. Blair moved to Dublin where he managed the only refinery in that city until his death in 1886.

15. Baker Street (at top of) – Patten's – the large refinery of Archibald Patten & Co 1848–1877.

16. Crescent Street – the first fireproof works in Scotland, opened by Wrede & Co in 1851 and worked to 1859. Became the Cartsburn Refining Co in 1862 and was run until the mid-1890s under various management, including John Aitken who is shown in the 1881 census as employing 195 men and 9 boys.

17. Drumfrocher Road – Berryyards Refinery – at the head of Lynedoch Street, it was started by Anderson, Orr & Co in 1852 with Alex Scott and W B Paul as partners and refiners. Alex Scott & Sons ran it from 1864 until 1896 when it was sold to the Brewers Sugar Co. This became Tate & Lyle's Westburn Refinery that ran right through to 1997.

18. Dellingburn Reservoir – 1853–1865, destroyed by fire.

19. Baker Street – an old logwood mill was converted into a refinery in 1858 by James Duncan and Alex Scott, but burned down within a year. A larger building took its place, but in 1866 Duncan moved to his new London refinery, leaving Baker Street to be worked by Alex Scott and Sons, but it was demolished a few years later.

20. Dellingburn Reservoir (directly opposite 18) – 1858–1895.

21. Ingleston Street – Paul, Sword & Co

started here in 1864, burned down in 1868, wound up in 1878. It became the Orchard Sugar Refining Company, run by the Cartsburn Refining Co, until 1889 when it was taken over by new management who ran it beyond the turn of the century using the same name.

22. Baker Street (at bottom of) – Deer Park Refinery – an old mill was converted in 1864 but was destroyed by fire two years later.

23. Drumfrochar Road – the refinery of Neill, Dempster and Neill, it was built in 1868 as a replacement for (18), and continued successfully into the 1900s.

24. Drumfrochar Road – Clyde Sugar Refining Co – an old Cotton Mill, it was converted in 1873 by Cowan, Oliphant & Livingston. It continued till 1889.

There were four refineries in Port Glasgow, the first opening in 1777, the last closing in 1867. Also the Fowler brothers were in Robert Street, Port Glasgow, from the late 1860s until they moved their company, which appears to have concentrated on treacle, to Orchard Place in Blackwall, Essex, sometime before 1890.

Greenock was the birthplace of James Watt, and it had most certainly benefited from his inventive skills and the industrial revolution in general. It may well have been a late-starter in the refining industry but, for such a small town, it definitely made up for it in the 19th century. In 1881 Greenock had 11 refineries running, with the census of that year showing more than 900 men employed in the trade. Some 500 were Irish labourers living in the terraces and tenements close to their places of work, and many of these had local-born sons working in the refineries too.

Berryyards Refinery, Greenock,
© McLean Museum & Art Gallery, Greenock

Hull...

In 1672, William Smith and William Catlin renegotiated with the Mayor and Burgesses of Hull the lease on their rape-seed mill on Trippet (now southern end of Wincolmlee) on the west bank of the River

Hull just up-river from North Bridge. Their previous lease had run from 1658 and they had only recently changed the use of their *"great building of brick"* from that of a sugarhouse.[23] There was also a second sugarhouse at around this time at the mouth of the river at South End.[24]

The industry was revived again in 1732. Robert Thornton, a wealthy London merchant with roots in Yorkshire, in partnership with Samuel Watson, a Hull merchant, and other members of both families as well as William Wilberforce, another Hull merchant and grandfather of the Abolitionist of the same name, built a large sugarhouse directly opposite Trippet on the east bank of the river in Lime Street. They traded as Thornton, Watson & Co. Production continued for more

than a century, with the Thornton family always at the helm but with a succession of refiners, including Joseph Rennard, John Hodgson and James Gadsden in charge of the day-to-day business.[25]

The refinery closed when Gadsden retired in 1840.[26] It became a seed warehouse, gaining national publicity in 1868 when half of it collapsed under the weight of its contents, killing seven workers and a young boy who was unfortunate enough to have been passing along Lime Street at the time.[27] Either side of 1800, there were two other sugarhouses on the River Hull – Bassano, Carlill & Co on Wincolmlee and G F Boyes further upriver on Church Street. The latter was built as the "New Sugar House" and had three tenements for workmen, but was up for sale by 1817

Old Sugar House Disaster, Hull, Illustrated London News, October 1868

owing to the bankruptcy of John Boyes.[28] The parish registers of Drypool, Sutton-on-Hull and Sculcoates show that there were a number of German sugarbakers working in Hull and worshipping locally. There was not a German church there until 1848. Nevertheless, both Samuel Thornton and John Boyes were concerned enough in 1802 to jointly apply to His Majesty's Justices of the Peace for Rev Christopher F Triebner, a Lutheran who had arrived in Hull from St Mary's in the Savoy, London, to be licensed *"to preach the Word of God to the Germans employed in their sugarhouses and others in Hull"*.[29]

It is suggested that there were several proposals and attempts in the second half of the 19th century to revive the industry in Hull yet again. These appear to have come to little, although as with most towns and cities there were a number of confectioners trading.[30]

Lancaster...

Both Lancaster's sugarhouses were in St Leonard's Gate. John Hodgson sold the first sugarhouse on St Leonardgate, with its brewhouse and warehouse, to John Lawson, a local merchant and Quaker, probably some time before 1680. Lawson built a bridge over the millstream, and in 1680 a wharf, Lawson's Quay, on the Green Ayre next to the River Lune.[31] We can assume that both of these were to allow the speedier movement of raw sugar to his sugarhouse from his ships returning from the West Indies. The 1684 map of Lancaster shows this sugarhouse midway along St Leonardgate and downstream from Lawson's Quay, and, I think, where the present Council Offices are situated.

In February 1766, Robert Foxcroft of Lancaster leased his sugarhouse further along St Leonard Gate to five Lancaster gentlemen namely Robert Lawson, Abraham Rawlinson, Henry Hargreaves, Miles Birkett and George Foxcroft, and Luke Astley, a grocer of Preston. The whole, possibly known as the Sugarhouse Company, was divided equally into six shares. In 1769, Lawson, Rawlinson and Hargreaves bought out Birkett and Foxcroft, and in 1772 Rawlinson and Hargreaves bought the Astley

share.[32] A directory entry of 1793–8 shows the refinery belonging to James Hargreaves, Henry's son. George Crossfield & Co are known to have been running the sugarhouse from 1827–1834.[33] The Lancaster maps of 1778, 1807, and 1824 show only this one sugarhouse towards the northern end of St Leonard Gate, and slightly upstream from Lawson's Quay. The sugarhouse complex appears to have stood midway between the present Phoenix Street and Germany Street, and stretched from St Leonard Gate back to Cable Street (now Parliament Street).

Both Heartwick Grippenhearl who was made a Freeman of Lancaster in 1748–9, and Johann Hinrich Holthusen who is listed in directories 1829–34, are known German sugar refiners in Lancaster,[34] as was Henry Ahrens, the nephew of George Lilkendey, the London refiner, his 1814 will having been witnessed by George and James Crossfield,[35] probably his employers.

Liverpool...

Imagine you've just walked up two steps to the front door of house no 6. A pallid gentleman who looks older than his 47 years opens it. He tells you, in poor English, that his name is John Cappell. You are invited into a room maybe 12 ft square, with one small window through which comes very little light, a crude flight of stairs and little furniture. To the front are the door and window, to the sides and rear the party walls of the adjoining terraced and back-to-back houses. The stairs lead to two bedrooms equal in size to the room in which you are standing, one above the other and each with one small window. Your host introduces you to his family – Dora his wife, sons John, Henry and Bernard, all German-born, and the two little ones Emma and William, both born in Cheshire, as well as his three German lodgers, each in his early twenties. John junior, who's picked up the language better than any of them, explains that his father, the three lodgers and himself all work at Macfie's sugar refinery in the same street, as do their Irish neighbours Peter McCoy next door at no 5 and Barney and his lodger James Crawford across at no 3.[36] The hours are long and they have to sleep, so you take your leave remembering that you have to find your way out to the street again. From the front door you see a similar terrace of three houses opposite, no more than 10 ft away. Down the steps to the muddy, filthy yard where half a dozen children are playing, enclosed all round by 3-storey houses, with the backs of the houses of the adjoining streets closing off both ends – it rarely sees sunlight. In one corner of the yard is a privy and in another a stinking midden, both of which serve all six houses. To return to Batchelor Street, you stumble through a low, narrow alley about 14 ft long – a dark tunnel sloping up to the street.

You've just visited real people who lived at House 6 Court 2 Batchelor Street on census day 1861. The sizes given for the court and the house may not be exact, but they would have been very similar. The six tiny houses in the court housed at least 41 people, of whom well over half were adults, mostly Irish, with only the very youngest of the children having been born in the city.

Liverpool was notorious for its courts; many towns and cities had them, but none were quite so widespread, overcrowded and insanitary. First built close to the centre of town around 1700, they spread wherever new streets were laid out. They were built between the rows of terraces in the spaces where we would expect gardens to be, or wherever land became available hidden away behind warehouses and factories. There was a move to have the practice stopped towards the end of that century, but it took until 1862. A series of informed articles in the Liverpool Daily Post in 1883 under the banner *"Squalid Liverpool"* should have helped, but it was well into the 20th century before mass clearance was undertaken.[37] The censuses show us that many refinery workers lived in these courts, and undoubtedly a greater proportion did so before 1841 when the sugarhouses were closer to the centre of Liverpool. The 19th century saw the new refineries built away from the centre, a few to the south, but mostly to the north on either side of Vauxhall Road. Names like Viccars in Eldon Place, Jager in Black

Diamond Street and Burlington Street, Leitch and Crossfield both in Blackstock Street, Tate in Earle Street and then Love Lane, and of course Fairrie in the refinery that actually bridged Vauxhall Road. The mile upon mile of terraces and courts in the likes of Burlington Street, Hopwood Street and Athol Street would have housed the workers.

Liverpool's first sugarhouses were established around 1670. The VCH quotes from Sir Edward Moore's Rental of 1667–8,[38] referring to a plot of land in Dale Street –

> *Sugar-House Close… This croft fronts the street for some twenty-seven yards and I call it the Sugar House Close, because one Mr Smith, a great sugar-baker at London, a man as report says, worth forty thousand pounds, came from London to treat with me. According to agreement he is to build all the front twenty-seven yards a stately house of good hewn stone… and there on the back side, to erect a house for boiling and drying sugar, otherwise called a sugar-baker's house… If this be once done, it will bring a trade of at least forty thousand pounds a year from the Barbadoes, which formerly this town never knew.*

Smith may have built there, though more likely close to "the Pool" near Redcross Street where Cleveland and Danvers set up at a similar time. By 1768 there were eight sugarhouses. Five of these are shown on George Perry's map of 1769: "Sugar House Yard" – north of the Old Dock and east of Old Strand Street, and the site of the presumed first sugar house; "Sugar House near the Pig Market" – in Redcross Street; "Sugar House in John Street" – now North John Street, on the corner of Harrington Street; "Sugar House in Argyle Street" – off Hanover Street southwards to the west of Duke Street; "Sugar House in the Hay Market" – roughly where Victoria Street now meets the tunnel entrance.[39]

Sugar refining grew rapidly with Liverpool's profitable connections to transatlantic shipping and the triangular trade, and by the time slavery was eventually abolished it was firmly established as one of the city's leading industries. The general decline in the trade in the second half of the 19th century saw the smaller businesses close just like those of other refining centres, but Liverpool's larger refiners continued to profit. When Henry Tate set up his Love Lane refinery in 1872 little did his competitors know what they were in for. Having also built a new refinery at Silvertown in London, when he died in 1899 he left a business that would go on to amalgamate with Lyle's in 1921, and acquire Jager's in 1925, Fairrie's in 1929 and Macfie's in 1938. Tate & Lyle's became such a landmark in Liverpool, and such a huge employer, that it's closure in 1981 caused large demonstrations with even the Roman Catholic Archbishop and the Anglican Bishop of Liverpool moved to attend meetings in support of the workers. Many will remember Alan Bleasdale's TV drama of that time, *"Boys from the Blackstuff"*, that highlighted the city's unemployment. In the closing scene Chrissy, Logo and Yosser "Gis a job" Hughes, are seen leaving a "redundancy party" at the Green Man and tramping disconsolately alongside the actual refinery walls behind which, ironically, the real-life demolition gangs can be seen hard at work.[40]

London...

Richard Horwood spent the best part of nine years of his life conducting his incredible survey of London, producing clear, large-scale maps the likes of which had not been seen before. He named prominent buildings, identified many businesses (eg. Mr Coslet's Sugar House), and showed almost every dwelling with its house number. His first edition was published gradually from 1790, but the 32-sheet project was not completed until 1799. Having received subscriptions from the Phoenix Fire Office, Horwood shaded those industrial premises that Phoenix insured, many of them sugarhouses. He died in 1803 and the plates for the maps were purchased by William Faden, who made a number of revisions and improvements over the years, with the 1813 edition being of most importance to us as it is available in book form today.[41] That set of maps, along with John

Lockie's gazetteer[42] of London streets for the same year, are invaluable to researchers of the period 30 years either side of 1800. For those researching the Victorian period, the Godfrey Editions of Old Ordnance Survey Maps,[43] eg. London Sheet 63, Whitechapel, Spitalfields and The Bank, 1873, are extremely useful, clearly showing the sugarhouses and the terraces in which the workers lived. I mention these maps as a primary source of information simply because they explain the working/living situation in London far better visually than I can in words.

London's refining trade undoubtedly began in the City and then spread generally eastwards, though those refineries south of the River Thames in Lambeth, Southwark, Bermondsey etc, should not be overlooked. At the start of the 18th century much of London's refining took place in the sugarhouses on, and to either side of, Upper Thames Street in the general area between St Paul's Cathedral and the river. Raw sugar would have been unloaded at the wharves and the heavy hogsheads moved up the narrow lanes by cart to Thames Street and onwards to the sugarhouses. Towards the end of that century, the boiling of sugar in the City was much frowned upon, probably because of the smell rather than safety, and the building of new sugarhouses was supposedly stopped although large newly-built refineries at both Broken Wharf and 44 Upper Thames Street were advertised in 1806.[44] For all refining to have been "beyond Aldgate" would have suited "the City" well, but it took a long time for that to happen. For example, Smith and Tyers were still refining at 203 Upper Thames Street in 1851.

By 1725, sugarhouses had begun to spring up to the east and northeast of the Tower, in the parishes of Whitechapel and St George's in the East, slowly at first, in Angel Alley, Buckle Street and Salt Petre Bank for example. Incidentally, the latter, now Dock Street, may well have been the site of the East End's last refinery building, for in 1980 the old bonded tea warehouse at 40 Dock Street was demolished, this having been a refinery from the early 1800s through to 1874.[45] Businesses spread throughout both parishes towards the almost rural Mile End, and along the river's edge to Wapping, Shadwell and Limehouse, mirrored by similar development on the opposite bank. So many streets in Whitechapel and St George's had refineries, but a few deserve special mention. Alie Street, just south of Whitechapel High Street and right in the heart of the trade, was where St George's German Lutheran Church was built along with its school. Surrounded by Germans, both living and working in the area, this was an ideal location for such an important support service for the German community. Bowman's huge refinery complex was there for much of the 19th century until it was auctioned in 1872 as warehousing. South from the centre of Alie Street ran Leman Street, the Upper Thames Street of the East End in sugar terms. Busy with refineries throughout the 18th century and most of the 19th, important names like Tielhen, Shum, Constantien, Rhode, Harbusch, Martineau, Gadsden and Goodhart all worked there. Turn left at the bottom of Leman Street, and just along Cable Street there was Wellclose Square on the right, with its Danish Church, later a school, in the middle. The Square was an important centre for the refiners for a similar period to Leman Street, with names like Dirs, Turquand, Arney, Holthouse, Wackerbarth, Witte and Wagener all leaving their mark there. 48 Wellclose Square had been a sugarhouse from at least the 1790s, and when it ceased trading as such in the 1870s was taken over by George Whybrow who ran it as a pickle factory.

Further east along Cable Street, running north was Christian Street with refineries of a somewhat later period. Begun around 1800, Kuck, Schroder and Martineau were the important names. The censuses show labourers living nearby in Ellen, Providence, Severne and Grove Streets. Martineau's at no 6 was advertised for sale in 1892, but never again refined sugar, probably leaving Schwier's at 39 Dunk Street, Mile End New Town, as the only East End refinery. Ernst Louis Victor Schwier, a Hanoverian, began the Dunk Street business in 1855 having

been in the London sugar industry for the previous 14 years. His sons Charles, Ernest and Walter Schwier took over in 1883, but wound up their partnership in 1896. They sold the concern to Martineau's, who ran it right through until 1961, though with an office address at the rear of the Dunk Street premises at 13 Kingward Street (King Edward Street). The first illustration in this book was taken outside that address, for when George Frederick Tutte, a foreman at Martineau's, wanted a photo of himself and "his boys" immediately after WWII he chose the factory, which had such fond memories for them all, as the location. They only lived across the street and regarded the factory as family – the workers' children played and went to school together; the wives and mothers worked in their homes surrounding the factory and spent meal breaks with their husbands when possible; many of the women and young girls had odd jobs in the factory cleaning up, preparing meals etc; and when one of the girls was to be married she was told by her parents to ask the foreman over her father for permission to marry a "bloke from America".[46] Such loyalty and sense of community appears to have pervaded the industry.

With the decline in the trade in the 1870s–80s, Liverpool was showing that survival depended upon large, new refineries with good access by road and water. Out on the Essex marshes at Silvertown, Duncan, Tate,

48 Wellclose Square, St George's in the East, © Lynda Whybrow

Lyle and Martineau began anew. Raw sugar arrived with ease right to their wharves, new roads were built to connect back into London for the distribution of the finished products, and new housing, schools and churches were built for the workers. This housing would eventually spread north and east to form the huge developments through East Ham to Dagenham, the mapping of which would have driven Horwood to employ more than a few assistants!

Manchester...

A very commercial city, specialising almost completely in cotton, Manchester appears to have forgotten its sugar industry. The rivers Irwell and Medlock, the Manchester Ship Canal and the Rochdale Canal all played their part in allowing the transport of raw sugar into Manchester from Liverpool and thus the development of a late-starting, but important, trade.

Originally, the present Quay Street was straight and derived its name from the quay at the end of it on the River Irwell. Just a few yards to the south of the quay, on Water Street, was a sugarhouse, probably that run by Samuel Norcott in the 1770s.[47] A respected refiner, in 1777 he was consulted regarding the viability of the Cuppins Lane Sugar House in Chester. He considered there was little hope of success and offered advice on the most economic way of closing the premises down, but the owner took no notice and there is no evidence of the business succeeding for more than a year or so more.[48] In 1788 the premises in Water Street is listed as the Sugar Baking Company.

For much of the second half of the 19th century, there were refineries towards the south in Oxford, Chester, New Wakefield, Lower Moseley and Portland Streets, and further north around the cathedral in Cannon Street and Corporation Street as well as in Chapel Street on the other side of the river in Salford. However it was Hanging Ditch, just east of the cathedral that was most important at this time to Manchester. Here was the Corn and Produce Exchange with its associated

chambers that, amongst others, housed the offices of the numerous sugar producers, brokers and merchants who traded in Manchester. These included names from further afield such as Finzel & Son, the Sankey Sugar Co and George Crossfield & Co.

Regarding where the workers lived the censuses are a disappointment as the enumerators, for the most part, did not indicate the labourers' trades, although a number of Salford addresses can be identified in the 1881 census.

Newcastle-under-Lyme...

Was well inland for a refining town, but well served by the Trent and Mersey Canal and the River Trent. The 1881 census shows the Victoria Sugar Refinery, operated by Leonard Abington, in London Road, just to the south east of the town centre. Abington himself was living out at Checkley at the time, but of the identifiable workers there were possibly 3 or 4 boilers, 6 or 7 labourers, a packer, a timekeeper, and 2 commercial travellers, the majority of whom lived in the streets nearby. Even today the first right off London Road is Refinery Street.

Newcastle upon Tyne...

Close to the River Tyne, Atkinson & Co refined on Quayside in 1778 and, at the same time, a little further up river, Forster & Co worked in The Close. 10 years later they were working together along with Rankin in The Close, which in 1801 was run by Rankin & Watson, and in 1811 by Doubleday & Easterby.[49] The trade directories also show Rudman, Clark, Carr & Co were refining in the 1790s.

Plymouth...

The refinery site in Mill Lane would have stood very central in old Plymouth. A site which some 250 years earlier had provided the garden for the house, in Saltash Street, of Sir Francis Drake, sometime later the Frankfort

Barracks, and just prior to the refinery, a tannery and vegetable garden. The Waste (Mill) Leat, capable of turning a mill wheel, provided the water supply and power throughout these years.

In the 1830s, James Bryant, who had already opened a starch factory on part of the site, revived the sugar refining industry that had declined at the end of the previous century.[50] One of the first works had been on the eastern side of Sutton Pool, and there was said to have been a round "cane grinding" building in Exeter Road.[51] By 1844 his refinery was insured for £5500 by the Phoenix Fire Office.[52] Partnership with Mr Burnell soon came, and in 1856 the refinery became the British and Irish Sugar Refining Company, with Bryant and Burnell appointed deputy chairmen. With business booming the town had four refineries with, at one point, the sugar duties accounting for half the Customs receipts for the Port. In 1886, however, the company became unprofitable and was put up for sale. In 1890 it was acquired by Sir Edward Bates MP, though he soon sustained heavy losses, and closed down.

From then on the site had various uses – shops, stables, clothing factory, builders' merchants, cooperage, telegraph stores, and furniture repository, as well as being the winter store for Hancock's fair and menagerie. Before WWII, one of the two 120ft chimneys was carefully demolished, but the Blitz soon claimed the largest of the buildings on the site.[53] With the centre of Plymouth destroyed by the bombing, in 1953 the site was in the way of the development of the town's new centre, and finished up beneath Mayflower Street and the car parks on either side of it.[54]

Sheffield...

Edward Bennet, a metal grinder by trade, went to London, married, learned how to refine sugar and returned to Sheffield to set up his own refinery at the bottom of Coalpit Lane. This may have been as early as 1737, and in 1778 he insured his substantial premises with Sun Fire Office for £4000.[55] He died in 1788.

There's evidence of Samuel Revell refining in Nursery Street from 1828–42[56], and John von Hollen in the same street prior to his death in 1842. Von Hollen's will[57] was witnessed by George Walker, sugar refiner, and he is listed in Exchange Street as Walker & Wall in 1852, and in 1862 as George Walker & Co[58]. Both locations were close to the River Don. Samuel Greaves is also shown in 1862 at Bacon Island in Effingham Lane[59], between the river and the canal.

Southampton[60]...

There is evidence of only one early sugarhouse in Southampton, built in about 1743, on the derelict site of the Friary, with easy access to the Town Quay and a ready supply of fresh water. Detailed excavation of the site in the 1970s by Southampton Museum of Archaeology revealed a rectangular sugarhouse, with evidence of boiling pans with ash pits, stoves, and a central cistern, and archived plans and documents show various other buildings on the site. Fragments of moulds and drip pots were found in the main refinery building and sealed into the surface of the yard, too few though to indicate a normal breakage rate, suggesting that sherds were either disposed of elsewhere or perhaps sold for road making.

John Brissault ran the sugarhouse for some 30 years until he was declared bankrupt in 1774, and by 1786 the building was being used as a granary. Evidence of use of the site and buildings shows that the Sugar House and Sugar House Lane retained their names until after WWII. The sugarhouse remained intact until the Blitz of 1940 and was finally demolished about 1942, with photographs taken at those times showing the building to have been of 7 storeys above ground. The site was built upon in 2001/2, providing prestigious flats, town houses and maisonettes. Something of what is left of the boundary walls has been preserved alongside the Gloucester Place car park.

Garton, Hill & Co produced sugar for brewing here from about 1847, before moving to London in 1882.[61]

Warrington[62]...

There was certainly one sugarhouse here, in two buildings – one the boiling house, the other the stables and storehouse – set one on each side of Sugar House Lane (now Bewsey Street) at the bottom of Horsemarket Street. The earliest reference is probably 1755, with an inventory available for 1768. In 1778, however, Robert Hesketh of Chester, and Joseph Parr and Richard Astley, both of Warrington, all described as merchants, bought the lease from Thomas Patten and John Leigh. Joseph Parr & Co continued through to about 1786, with Hesketh retiring in 1781. The sugarhouse was insured with the Sun Fire Office in 1778 for £3000, rising to £5000 in 1782, then down to £2000 in 1786. Parr's brother-in-law, Thomas Lyon, in partnership with John Winckleman, insured a second sugarhouse for £2000 in 1778, but there is no mention of its location.

When the downturn in trade beset their small sugarhouses, Joseph Parr, Thomas Lyon and Walter Kerfoot became founder members of Warrington's first bank, Parr & Co, in 1788, which would eventually grow into the Westminster Bank.

Whitehaven...

Duke Street and Scotch Street were where sugar was produced in the 1820s according to contemporary trade directories. Johnson & Manley refined in Duke Street in 1821 followed by Edward Johnson & Co, with the latter also refining at 4 Scotch Street in 1829.[63] Meanwhile, both Edward Johnsons, senior and junior, were declared bankrupt in 1826.[64]

With the huge competition from Liverpool just down the coast, it is likely the production was small and for local consumption. Nevertheless, there is much earlier evidence of sugar arriving at Whitehaven,[65] the original sugarhouse in Duke Street having been commissioned by the Lowther family in 1712.[66]

Also...

Dundee had a sugar refining company from 1751; Raisbeck, Grey, Burden & Co were refining in Stockton-on-Tees in 1784; and Chambers in Gloucester 1799. Some time later, on the banks of the River Ouse at Goole, Mr A Maude was refining in the 1840s and maybe for much longer, as the will of George Christian Schilling of Goole dated 1871 shows his occupation to have been "manager at sugarhouse". Pottery finds, which include sherds of sugar moulds and drip pots, have been found in both Exeter and Belfast, and it is also suggested that the Whitehaven trade may have spread to nearby Workington. All of these, however, and maybe other towns, require further research.

*   *   *

But what of the owners or lessees of the refineries? Whilst their employees moved as close as possible to their work, the owners of the businesses, given the financial wherewithal, moved in the opposite direction to leafy Surrey or the open spaces of Essex, and to the countryside around the other refining centres. This, at least, would have been the aim of many owner-refiners, but at first it would have been a matter of living "over the shop" for some years whilst their businesses developed, and very many did not get beyond that. There was many a bankruptcy in this trade, but those who could afford to would have eventually employed a manager, who may have been the master boiler, to run the sugarhouse leaving them free to move further away and travel in when they wished. Of the London refiners, eg Edward Blamire of Epping, George Dettmar of Wanstead, and Henry Engell of West Ham and, to the south, David Martineau of Stockwell, George Shum Storey of Ham Common, Ludwig Witte of Clapham Rise, Jacob Goodhart of Streatham and Conrad Wohlgemuth of Hollington, near Hastings, Sussex. Elsewhere we find John W Macfie, the Liverpool refiner, at Lower Bebington in Cheshire, whilst Conrad Finzel lived at Frankfort Hall outside Bristol and James

McNair built the fine villa of Calder Park, about four miles east of Glasgow. There were also those partners in refining businesses who were not refiners but merchants or ship owners, and it was probably rare for them to go near their investments, let alone live near them.

Their investments were bricks and mortar, utensils and stock, with the average set-up costs in mid-eighteenth century London of £1000–£5000,[67] borne out by Sun Fire Office valuations for that time ranging from £200 to £5000.[68] In 1783, Chambers Cyclopaedia suggested probable sizes for the buildings –

Sugar house, is a brick or stone building, constructed for a sugar refinery manufactory. A house intended to contain one or two pans should be square or nearly square: but a house of larger dimensions ought to be of an oblong form; as it may be conveniently heated, by placing the chimney of the stove and of the pans at opposite angles. A house to contain one pan should consist of six floors besides the ground floor; the dimensions about twenty seven feet square: the two pan house about thirty six feet by forty feet: a house of four pans about forty feet by sixty or sixty five feet. The stove is a brick building from eight to fourteen feet square, usually placed in one corner of the building. The height of the several stories should be as follows: the fill house, or the ground floor, nine feet below the girders; the next floor above it, called the warehouse, of the same height: and every other floor upwards, six feet at most between the girders and floor. In every floor must be left an aperture, through which a rope is suspended upon a brass pulley on the uppermost floor for drawing up the sugar; and provided due attention be given to the strength of the building, and to the exclusion of damps and a cold air, a sugar house cannot be rendered too light. (The notorious "aperture in every floor" caught out many, as we shall see later.)

The King Street sugarhouse in Glasgow, sold in 1790, fitted the bill exactly being 63 ft x 41 ft and 6 floors high,[69] whilst the Rhinelander sugarhouse in New York was another good example, being maybe 60 ft x 40 ft, 6 floors plus garret, with 16 windows to each floor. It

was built in 1763 and demolished in 1892. In Back Church Lane, Whitechapel, a new sugarhouse was built, probably for John Hodgson about 1810, measuring a simple 54 ft square.[70] The earlier Southampton house of 1743 was somewhat larger, however, for it appears to have had only three, maybe four, pans but had two stoves, was about 85 ft x 45 ft and 7 floors high. Like most, it also had associated cooperage, raw sugar store, sugar mill, and dwelling house.[71]

When Robert & James McNair moved house in Glasgow around 1800, it was described thus, *"This new sugar house stood as a very prominent object many years. It was a huge clumsy-looking edifice of four storeys, fronting both Ingram and Queen Streets, the entrance being from the latter. There were rows of small square windows, and the whole building was very dingy from its smoke."*[72] So sugarhouses were "huge piles of buildings" a long, long time before Dickens described them as such.

Access to a continuous supply of water was essential. Bristol's second sugarhouse at St Augustine's Back eventually failed when the City Corporation restricted its supply from nearby Brandon Hill in favour of the local community.[73] London refiners were treated much better in the terrible winter of 1814, for the East London Water Company congratulated itself in *The Times* of 28 January for having kept up the supply of water to the sugar refineries.[74]

With as many windows as possible, lighting may not have been too much of a problem in daylight hours but work always started in the early hours and in the winter would have gone on until dark. The 1690 inventory for Whitson Court, Bristol, shows 32 dozen candles at 4s 6d a dozen and 9 candlesticks valued at 1s.[75] An observer at a London refinery some 180 years later commented on the gloom with *"here and there a foggy little gas-jet burning blear-eyed against the wall"* and *"lit with gas just enough to show all manner of wriggling and revolving machinery overhead and threading the walls"*.[76] Heating was never a problem, though it needed controlling, as Chambers Cyclopaedia continues –

After all, a principal consideration in the construction of a sugar house, is the obtaining of a sufficient degree of heat. Various degrees of heat are required for different sorts of goods, and occasionally for the same sort: accordingly each floor may be made more or less warm as the case requires. The heat is introduced through the pan chimney, the stove chimney, and sometimes through iron or brick flues raised on purpose. It is communicated from the chimneys by shutting the register-plates, after the fires are extinguished, or when they are nearly out, and the remaining ashes are perfectly clear. After shutting the register-plates, the small iron doors (one of which is fixed in the chimneys both of the cockell and the pans upon every floor) are opened, to convey heat where it is wanted.

Labourers in sugar houses are very subject to dysentries: the vitrum antimonii ceratum is an effectual remedy in these cases.

As demand grew so did production, and the refineries became larger, more often than not by attaching a second, and sometimes a third, sugarhouse to the original with thick fire doors giving access on each floor. On 27 September 1794 the lease of a large sugarhouse in Old Gravel Lane, Wapping, probably that of Camden, Lear & Thellusen, insured for £9500 with Sun, was advertised for sale in *The Times* with a description – "*a compact well-built sugar house six storeys high consisting of a large warehouse, a 4-pan single house, a 2-pan double house, a 2-pan scum house,*

Elevation of a Sugar Refinery, Robert Niccol, 1864

well secured by strong party walls between each, a counting house adjoining, brewhouse, cooperage, good stabling, and other detached offices" – showing just that arrangement, with the double house probably taking its name from the process of double refining the sugar. Similarly, Dettmar's in Osborn Street in 1823 had four houses of 3, 2, 1 and 2 pan capacity, and in 1833 at Guinea Street, Bristol, probably Rankin's, had a 7-pan house and a 5-pan house.

When steam engines were introduced, engine houses, boiler houses and chimneys were added, the latter often dwarfing the sugarhouses. Dames & Son of Osborn Street had a "handsome octagonal chimney shaft 150 ft high", though that of Martineau's in Christian Street was apparently taller. From 1813 onwards, the slow but sure replacement of open boiling pans with vacuum pans, and the associated pipe work and improved filtering systems, caused considerable disruption within existing sugarhouses. This new equipment was larger than the old and often required holes to be cut into walls and ceilings in order to accommodate it. New refineries were designed around the increasingly large vacuum pans that soon pierced two floors thus taking up space on three, usually central, floors.[77]

Some plans still exist for sugarhouses. When John Wagener considered extending his London premises at 27 Wellclose Square around 1851 he had plans drawn up by C Dyson – surveyor.[78] Reflecting the existing building, the addition was to be 6 storeys above ground with a basement to hold two large boilers. The plans show concrete foundations, 23 inch thick brick walls for the basement and ground floor with 18 inch brick walls above, and the wooden floors, 24 ft square, were to be supported by six evenly spaced posts on each floor. Given the incredible heat the men had to work in, the ceiling heights were very low – only the ground floor exceeded 8ft, with the first floor at 7 ft 9 in, the second and third floors at 7 ft 4 in and the fourth and fifth floors at 7 ft – mostly less than that of your living room. On each floor there were to be three small windows on each external wall, with little or no ventilation as that would have made it more difficult to maintain the temperatures required for the various processes. Fireproof iron doors were to connect each new floor to the existing premises.

Strong, solid buildings these may have been but, as was found at Hull, the old sugarhouses built with wooden beams and floor joists were susceptible to movement and deterioration from the heat, and could not withstand the huge weight of the new equipment and the much-increased quantities of sugar being processed at any one time. Iron structural framing was developed to overcome these problems. William Fairbairn wrote in the late 1860s,

I have had several opportunities of testing the value of wrought-iron beams; and in proof of their greater security and adaptation for building such as mills, warehouses, etc, where great weights have to be supported, I have selected… a sugar refinery, and the weights these floors and beams have to sustain, when loaded with moist sugar, has been calculated at 400 lbs on a square foot, and the breaking weight of the beams is computed at 106 tons equally distributed. This building is probably one of the most important yet constructed with arches in wrought-iron beams, and we here refer to it as an example of what may be done by the introduction of a material free from flaws and much lighter than cast iron… the building is about 150 ft long and 58 ft wide with only one row of columns down the centre of the main building.[79]

These were indeed substantial buildings, and too good to be demolished when the industry had no further need for them. Most were used for general warehousing and often demolished when the area they were in was redeveloped but some, as we have seen, had long lives as specialist warehouses, granaries and even a hotel.

When Herman Almeroth managed to get enough pennies together to open his own sugarhouse in about 1809, he found a small plot, or perhaps a recently built sugarhouse, just north of the Whitechapel Road in Church Street (now Hanbury Street), Mile End New Town.

Location of sugarhouse at 12 Church Street, Mile End New Town

The old Deal Street School, Mile End New Town, © Bryan Mawer

Horwood's first edition map does not show it, but the revised edition of 1813 does. By studying maps of the immediate area from 1746 to the present, it is possible to work out the exact location of the sugarhouse as there is still to be seen today a boundary line which the sugarhouse abutted dating back to before it was built. The original small sugarhouse stood where the arched entrance to the right of the old Deal Street School, now a community centre, is today.

I have no details of Herman's sugarhouse other than its exact location, but after his time it grew and grew in the hands of Burnell & Giess and then Dakin & Bryant, before it eventually closed leaving, like almost every other one that has ever existed in this country, absolutely no trace of itself on the ground.

Notes

1   Document TH4174 – Tower Hamlets Local History Library.
2   *The Times* 3 June 1882.
3   *The East End of London* by Millicent Rose, Cresset Press, 1951.
4   *Bristol and the Sugar Trade* by Alison Grant, Longman, 1981.
5   *The Port of Bristol, 1848–1884* by David Large, Bristol Record Soc, 1984.
6   *Bristol's Sugar Trade and Refining Industry* by Donald Jones, Bristol Branch of the Historical Assoc, 1996.
7   Bristol Record Office 36772 Box 3.
8   Jones (note 6).
9   Jones (note 6).
10 The late Mr I V Hall was a diligent researcher into the sugar trade in Bristol. Among his published works are those in the "Transactions of the Bristol & Gloucestershire Archaeological Soc – Vols. 65, 68, 74, 76, 80, 84, 85". His mass of unpublished research work is at Bristol Record Office under Ref: 36772.
11 Jones (note 6).
12 Cheshire and Chester Archives & Local Studies CCALS D/HINCKS.
13 Wilson's Dublin Directories.
14 *Notes on the Sugar Industry of the United Kingdom* by John M Hutcheson, James McKelvie, 1901.
15 Williamson's Edinburgh Directories.
16 *Sugar Refining Families of Great Britain* by G Fairrie, London: Tate & Lyle. 1951.
17 Hutcheson (note 14).
18 Gilhooley's 1752 Edinburgh Directory.
19 "Old Sugar House, 138 Gallowgate c1846" by William Simpson, at Provand's Lordship, Glasgow.
20 Hutcheson (note 14).
21 Hutcheson (note 14).
22 *History of Greenock* by R M Smith, Orr, Pollock & Co., Sugarhouse Lane, Greenock 1921.
23 Hull City Archives, M688, BRN/384–5.
24 Victoria County History – Yorkshire.
25 Lambeth Archives, IV/104/1–7.
26 *Some Aspects of Hull in the 19th Century – Business History – Pt. 1* by Joyce Bellamy, 1965, Hull Central Library.
27 The Hull & Eastern Counties Herald, 1 Oct 1868; Illustrated London News, Oct 1868.
28 Hull Advertiser & Exchange Gazette, 26 Apr 1817.
29 *The Hull German Lutheran Church* by Barbara Robinson, Highgate Pub, 2000.
30 Bellamy (note 25).
31 *Lancaster – A History* by Andrew White, Phillimore, 2003. ISBN 1-86077-244-7.
32 Manchester Archives & Local Studies – Refs : L245, L246, L247.
33 1) Pigot's Dir 1828–9. 2) White (note 30).
34 White (note 30).
35 The National Archives PROB 11/1553, 1814.
36 1861 census RG9/2667/112.
37 *Liverpool – Our City, Our Heritage*, Freddy O'Connor, 1990.
38 Moore Rental (Chetham Soc. Remains, xii), 76–78. (Victoria County History – Lancaster).
39 *Liverpool's Place in the History of Sugar Refining*, Neville H King, 1997/2000.
40 *Boys and Girls from the Whitestuff*, Ron Noon, 2001.
41 "The A to Z of Regency London", London Topographical Society, Pub. No 131, 1985.
42 "Topography of London, facsimile of John Lockie's Gazetteer 1813", London Topographical Society, Pub. No 148, 1994.
43 "Old Ordnance Survey Maps", Alan Godfrey Maps, Gateshead.
44 The National Archives C217/61.
45 1) *Essex and Sugar*, Frank Lewis, Phillimore, 1976. 2) Mrs C Ely (photo THL).
46 Jane E Tutte Mayberry, 2006.

47   Manchester & Salford Directories 1772 & 1788.

48   Cheshire and Chester Archives & Local Studies CCALS D/HINCKS/73.

49   Bristol Record Office 36772 Box 5.

50   *Western Morning News*, Thursday, September 18, 1952.

51   Ref P664.1, Plymouth Local Studies Library.

52   Cambridge University Library – PX513.

53   *Western Morning News* (note 50).

54   *Plan for Plymouth.*

55   *Indexes of the Fire Insurance Policies of the Sun Fire Office and the Royal Exchange Assurance, 1775–87* by D T Jenkins.

56   1) The National Archives DEL 10/149. 2) BRO 36772 Box 3.

57   The National Archives PROB 11/1963.

58   1) Sheffield Directory 1852. 2) BRO 36772 Box 3.

59   Bristol Record Office 36772 Box 3.

60   *Sugar Refining in Southampton* by J.C.Drake of Southampton Museum of Archaeology, 1987.

61   *1855–1955: A hundred years of progress – Manbré & Garton Ltd*, by J L Garbutt.

62   1) "Sugar Refining – another of Warrington's lost trades", *Warrington Guardian* 7 Nov 1936. 2) *Indexes of the Fire Insurance Policies of the Sun Fire Office and the Royal Exchange Assurance, 1775–87* by D T Jenkins.

63   *Principal Inhabitants of Cumberland & Westmoreland.*

64   Society of Genealogists Lists of Bankrupts.

65   *Coal and Tobacco 1660–1700* by J V Beckett, CUP, 1981.

66   *Whitehaven 1660–1800*, Royal Commission on the Historical Monuments of England, 1991.

67   *The Making of the English Middle Class (London 1660–1730)*, by Peter Earle, Methuen, 1989.

68   Guildhall Library – Sun Fire Office Insurance Policies.

69   *The Glasgow Mercury*, 22–29 Jun 1790.

70   London Metropolitan Archives Plan THCS/P3/82A.

71   Drake (note 60).

72   *The old country houses of the old Glasgow gentry*, John Guthrie Smith and John Oswald Mitchell, 1878.

73   *Bristol's Second Sugar House*, I V Hall, BGAS, Transactions, 1949, Vol 68.

74   *London in the Age of Industrialisation: Entrepreneurs, labour force and living conditions, 1700–1850*, L D Schwarz, CUP, 1992.

75   Chancery Proceedings, Bridges Division, Bundle 192/24, 1690 – Bristol Record Office 36772 Box 5.

76   *The Wilds of London* by James Greenwood, 1876.

77   *Sugar – A Handbook for Planters & Refiners*, Lock, Newlands & Newlands, pub Spon, 1888.

78   London Metropolitan Archives – MBO/PLANS/440–2.

79   *On the application of cast and wrought iron to building purposes*, William Fairbairn, 4th ed 1870.

THE ROPE

Michael Schopman recalls being told that his grandfather always had a rope under the bed, in case of fire. For many years this meant nothing to him, but now the significance has become clear...his grandfather was brought up amongst the sugar refineries in Whitechapel, and his great grandfather, a German, worked in one.

What did they do?

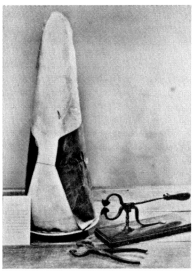

19th century Sugar Loaf and Cutters, © Cambridge & County Folk Museum

Herman Almeroth died in May 1812, aged 50, and was buried in the churchyard of St Dunstan Stepney, the cause of death unrecorded. The burial registers give no hint and it was too early for there to have been a death certificate. To die at this early age was not unusual in this trade: the hours were long, conditions appalling and accidents aplenty. Whilst many sugarbakers got out of the job and took on less arduous work, those that did stay must have found it very, very difficult to prolong their lives into old age. They were said to be *"liable to pulmonic disorders and rheumatism… become sallow, emaciated and dropsical and die at an early period of life"*.[1] In 1841, G Dodd wrote a long article for the *Penny Magazine*[2] about the processes of refining and the conditions the men worked in. Some 30 years later James Greenwood visited a refinery, long after Herman's death and well into the decline of the East End trade, even then the conditions he found he could not really believe. His wonderfully graphic descriptions from "The Wilds of London", 1876, say more about the conditions the men worked in than the processes involved…

Regarding the mild and innocent-looking sugar-lump, so pure, and bright, and sparkling, it is by no means easy to believe how its production can involve any prodigious amount of hard labour and man-sweating; so it is, however. Accidentally it came to my knowledge just recently that the manufacture of the saccharine luxury – a branch of trade of considerable importance, and providing with employment several thousand men at the east-end of London alone – was looked on, on account of its excessive hardship, with such dislike, that even that pattern of patient drudgery, the Irish labourer, could by no sort of persuasion be brought to undertake it. I was credibly informed that the bribe offered had taken even the seductive form of beer unlimited; but that still, marvellous to relate, the Emerald Islander remained obdurate, and the sugar-bakers were compelled, as has ever been the case, to resort for "hands" to the German labour market. There appeared to me something so unaccountable about this last feature of the business, that I resolved to go and find how it came about. I cannot give the name of the bakery selected, as I have clean forgotten it; but the reader will be at no loss on that score, since I was given to understand that one system regulates the business, and that one bakery is as much like another as peas of a pod. It is by no means a hole-and-corner business, as one might be led to imagine it was, judging from the rare occasions of its being brought under public notice. In the neighbourhood of Back-church-Lane, in Whitechapel, there are dozens of these baking, or, as they would more properly be called, boiling-houses. They are buildings enormous in size, usually occupying the whole of a street side, and so high that the massy "mats" of sugar craned up to the topmost story, and there dangling from its chains, looks no bigger or more substantial than a fishmonger's rush-basket that the wind might blow away.

A kind-hearted German missionary was my companion, and soon as I put my head in at the door of the bakery, the nature of the manufacture in progress was at once made apparent to my senses. Just as unmeasured indulgence in sugar is nauseating to the palate, so was the reek of it palling to one's sense of smell. You could taste its clammy sweetness on the lips just as the salt of the sea may be so discovered while the ocean is yet a mile away.

It was a sort of handy outer warehouse, that to which we were first introduced – a low-roofed, dismal place with grated windows, and here and there a foggy little gas-jet burning blear-eyed against the wall. The walls were black – not painted black. As far as one might judge they were bare brick, but "basted" unceasingly by the luscious steam that enveloped the place, they had become coated with a thick preserve of sugar and grime. The floor was black, and all corrugated and hard, like a public thoroughfare after a shower and then a frost. The roof was black, and pendent from the great supporting posts and balks of timber were sooty, glistening icicles and exudings like those of the gum-tree. "Sugar, sugar everywhere, but not a bit to eat." Exactly the Bogeydom to which should be consigned for a term, according to the degree of their iniquity, the owners of larcenous little fingers so persistent in their attacks on the domestic sugar-basin. At the extremity of this gloomy cave, and glowing duskily at the mouth of a narrow passage, was dimly visible a gigantic globular structure in bright copper, and hovering about it a creature with bare arms and chest all grizzly-

haired, with a long bright rod of iron in his grasp, which incessantly he waved about the mighty caldron; this was doubtless the Sugar Ogre himself, in waiting for juvenile delinquents.

Being in no dread of the ogre, however, we approached him, and discovered him to be a very civil fellow, quietly minding his business. The copper structure above-mentioned proved to be nothing more necromantic than a gigantic pan, in which were, gently seething, ten tons of liquid sugar. The vessel was all covered in, and looked as compact as an orange, the shape of which fruit it resembles ; but in the side of it there was a small disc of glass, and looking through it one could get a glimpse of the bubbling straw-coloured mass within. The iron rod the guardian of the pan called a "key," if I rightly remember, and his sole occupation appeared to consist in dipping it in at a little hole in the vessel's side, and withdrawing it again, along with a little blob of melted sugar, which he took between his finger and thumb, and drew out and examined by the light of the gas.

From this we were conducted to the factory where the manufacturers of moist sugar were working. It may appear strange to the reader that the term "manufacture" should be applied to what every schoolboy knows to be a natural production, but it is by no means an incorrect term notwithstanding. Some sugars are prepared at the place of their growth, and sent here ready for immediate use; but the great bulk of it is exported in a very rough state, dense, strong smelling, and of the colour of mahogany, and before it can be brought to assume the bright and inviting appearance it bears when ticketed in the grocer's window it has to undergo much torture by fire and machinery.

It was not a nice-looking place that to which we were introduced. It was not a pleasant way that led to it, inasmuch as it was in an underground direction, and through passages gloomy, low-roofed, and narrow, and lit with gas just enough to show all manner of wriggling and revolving machinery overhead and threading the walls. Down we went, however – our conductor kindly making the passage safer by illumining it by means of an old newspaper hastily twisted into a torch, and there we were in full view of the makers of moist sugar.

The fullest possible view under the circumstances, it should have been written, for a clear view was impossible; which, as we presently discovered, was a matter to be thankful for rather than to regret; horrors bursting suddenly on the unprepared vision have a bad effect sometimes. The place was nothing but a vast cellar underground, and lit from without only by a window here and there high up where the street pavement was, and as closely grated as though it were an object to keep flies out of the factory. The heat was sickening and oppressive, and an unctuous steam, thick and foggy, filled the cellar from end to end. Presently, however, when one's eyes grew some what accustomed to the gloom, a spectacle of a novel and startling character was presented. Seeming, as it were, to grow out of the dense haze, busy figures appeared. Black and white figures running about, and flitting and skipping in the most extraordinary manner. Watching the figures, however, they were presently discovered to be men in a condition of at least semi-nudity. On one side of the cellar were two gigantic pans of sugar, melted and hot and smoking, and out of these the labourers, naked but for a covering for their legs and some sort of apron, and their bodies bathed in sweat, and their fair hair reeking and hanging lank about their wan faces, scooped up the liquor into the pails, that would contain half a hundred weight, and hurried across the cellar to deposit it in vast revolving basins set in motion at lightning speed by machinery, and where the brown sugar was bleached and dried, to be presently shovelled out and added to the great heap that reached high nearly as the ceiling. Regarding the close, reeking, stifling place, the disgusting atmosphere, the incessant toil (machinery will not wait), and the disgusting conditions of it, the validity of the Irish labourer's objection became manifest; better a hod of bricks with a sixty-rung ladder to mount out in the open air than such mean, enervating drudgery as this. "They'd be dead without their beer unlimited," remarked our guide. "And does it not hurt them ?" "Well, it helps to knock them off, I dare say." So that it amounts to the same thing, only that the unlimited beer-drinker of the sugar bakery has the advantage of lengthy dying.

Out of this cellar and through others

similarly occupied, and then upstairs, and here to be sure was another strange sight. This was a branch of the loaf-sugar department. It was an extensive floor, a hundred feet by seventy probably, and covering the whole of it were packed loaf-sugar moulds as closely as the cells of a beehive are arranged. The moulds were stuck point downwards into earthen jars that at once upheld them and served as receptacles for their "drainings". I do not understand the process that was then operating, but what was to be seen was a dozen men of the semi-naked sort, like those below crawling like frogs over the surface of the sugar moulds, getting foot and hand hold on the edges, some with a sort of engine hose squirting a transparent liquor into the moulds, and others stirring the thick stuff constantly in the latter with their hands. "I should imagine that you were not much addicted to the consumption of sugar," I remarked to our guide. "I can never taste it; it has no taste no more, has nothing for me," he answered; and one could easily understand how that happened.

Upstairs, again, up crystallized stairs, with "toffee" for a handrail and hardbake to knock your head against if you were not aware of impending beams, to a room likewise full of moulds (they turn out twelve thousand loaves a week at this establishment), but where the greatest novelty to the eye of the uninitiated are many heaps of what in appearance is the exact counterpart of mud off the public roads. It was not so, however, as the guide explained it; it was merely the scrapings of beams and the shovellings of floors, and gangways, and workshops, and it was intended for filtration through charcoal, after which it would be deemed worthy to take its place as a marketable commodity.

Upstairs again – the place seemed to grow hotter the higher we climbed; and here was the "filling" department the place where the moulds were filled with liquid sugar, that flowed out of great taps. This, it seemed, was the hardest part of the sugar-baking business. Like every hand in the establishment, with the exception of the foreman and overlookers, the labourers here were midway nude (the disgusting practice is evidently one of habit rather than necessity amongst German sugar-bakers; we saw in one room – a comparatively cool room – half a dozen fellows squatted down engaged in the not over-heating occupation of painting moulds, but they were as naked as the rest). The moulds, as we were informed, when filled with the melted sugar, weigh a hundred-weight and a half, and the liquid, as it runs, is hot. The task to be performed is to fill the moulds at the taps and carry them across the great warehouses and arrange them close together for "setting," each in its own jar in the manner already described. A gang of a dozen or so are so employed, and as the work is piece work, hurry is the order of the day. But hurry is not easy with a hundredweight and a half of sloppy hot sugar to carry in an inconvenient vessel, and the result is that as they shuffle off in line with their loads there are many lurches, and stumblings, and elbowings, and the contents of the moulds hugged to the chest slop over the naked bodies of the carriers, and then harden and crust to a coat, doubtless as inconvenient to wear as it is disgusting to behold.

No wonder that the poor wretches so employed drink much beer. With no more exertion than leisurely walking about demanded, before I had been in the factory a quarter of an hour, I was drenched with perspiration, and was not a moment free from a trickling down my face. To be sure, since indulgence in beer assists the sugar-baker in his work it is commendable in the master to provide it. But, as I am informed, it is in his power to carry his kindness a step further – he can abridge the sugar-baker's labouring hours. The poor fellow's wages are quite as low as those of the Irish hodman, but, unlike the last-mentioned, he knows nothing of a "nine hours" law. The sugar-baker works all hours. What he calls a fair day's work is twelve hours, but it is not rare for him to be kept at the slavery above described for sixteen, and even eighteen hours – from three o'clock in the morning till eight at night – without a penny of overtime or extra pay. He cannot help himself. If he leaves one factory he must enter another exactly similar. It is a sight, I am told, to meet a group of the poor fellows just hurried from their beds, and making haste to their work at three o'clock of a winter's morning. Unrested, shivering, pale, and aguish, they are eager to get back to the heat and the beer; they need "warming up," as they say, and that object

effected, they manage to potter through the weary day somehow, and then they shuffle home to bed, and so on between Sunday and Saturday. The only time, my good missionary friend informed me – and he should know – when you can catch sight of a sugar-baker neither abed nor at work is on a Sunday afternoon, when he enjoys the luxury of idleness and a pipe at his own door or window.

These were the conditions described in the declining trade of the East End, and we can only hope that the more recently built refineries in Liverpool, Greenock and, more to the point, those of Silvertown, gave greater consideration to the workforce. It does beg the question, however, what the working conditions were like in the sugarhouses 100 years, even 200 years earlier. For until steam was introduced in the early 1800s, followed soon after by the vacuum pan, all sugar was boiled in open pans over open fires! Of course, we should also remember that the working conditions on the cane plantations in the Caribbean, without which the whole trade would not have existed, were no better.

A perennial grass and sweet to the taste, sugar cane originated in the South Pacific, probably New Guinea,[3] and was over the centuries taken across the world and bred to improve its sweetness and its suitability for the prevailing climates of each country. From the Pacific islands through India and China, across the Middle East to the Mediterranean islands and many African countries; then the Atlantic islands (the municipal seal of Funchal, the capital of Madeira, was formed from two canes complete with roots and leaves, and in between and on either side of them were conical loaves of sugar[4]) across to South America and most famously the Caribbean, then eventually to the southern states of the USA and finally Australia. Round the globe full circle and why – just because it tasted nice!

So easy to grow by simply laying a short length of stalk onto damp ground in the sunshine and almost watching it shoot and root, native growers enjoyed the wild plant simply to chew on, whilst it was considered invaluable by apothecaries as a medicine. As soon as the juices were extracted in quantity and boiled to produce a moist "sugar" it was considered a new "confection" by the courts and nobility and, although expensive, a "must-have" demand was established and thus began the sugar refining industry.

The insatiable demand for a product for which the human body has no need in its refined man-made form, which rots the teeth and contributes to illness and obesity, may never be quenched no matter what is put in its way. Aside from the health factors which ought to have brought individuals and nations to their senses by now, it is argued that the slave trade probably consumed 20 million native Africans, of which two-thirds could be charged against sugar,[5] before its eventual though reluctant abolition. The traditional cane-growing countries, by today's standards organic, were soon in decline as sugar beet was introduced and grown throughout Europe. New plantations of sugar cane were established in Queensland and Florida, all of which would be unsustainable without huge applications of artificial fertilizers, the run-off from which does the land, the watercourses and eventually the sea, no good whatsoever. Today's trade treaties and world business practices give the major producers, particularly those of sugar from beet, large subsidies to over-produce. It then allows them to sell their excess on the world market at low rates thus depressing prices to the detriment of the small producers of which many, ironically, just happen to be small African countries still struggling to survive.[6]

There is little evidence of sugar refiners being directly connected to the slave trade, although it has to be admitted a few partnerships that traded as sugar refiners also had within them partners who were owners of ships that both traded with the West Indies and were used as slave ships. Whilst the refiners clearly benefited from a ready supply of raw materials because of the slave trade, only a very few early families, particularly in Bristol, owned plantations. Raw sugar was shipped

to our islands from those of the West Indies in huge quantities – a ship full of good slaves could buy a number of ships full of sugar – and the refiners would have purchased their raw sugar from the wharfs several tons at a time, probably through brokers. But just what did they purchase?

The sugar arrived at the docks as a moist brown granulated substance packed into hogsheads (very large wooden barrels holding about 1/2–3/4 ton each) which often leaked dark molasses from their joints.

In a good crop of sugar cane, each stalk would have averaged about 12 ft in height, and weighed about 7 lbs. During growth the juices within had various compositions and purposes, but when fully ripe would have changed to sucrose with a sugar content of 15%.[7] The cane would have been cut and, before it began to deteriorate, moved quickly to the crushing mill – a set of two or three large solid rollers turned by men or mules, wind or water – through which the stalks (and occasionally an unfortunate operator) would have been drawn, squeezing out all the juices. These were then boiled in a succession of some half a dozen separate pans or cauldrons, the first containing up to 350 gallons and then decreasing in size.

Many of the impurities were removed by the addition of lime, and the liquid reduced to about half its volume before being allowed to crystallize. It was then set aside for some weeks for much of the molasses to drain out,

Boiling House, Useful Arts, 1846

before being packed into the hogsheads for transfer to the ports and shipment to Europe as muscovado sugar. Nothing was wasted on the plantations. The cane plant would sprout again to produce the following year's crop and sections of selected stalks replanted to produce new plants. The fibre, "bagasse", resulting from the crushing process would be used as fuel in the boiling house and generally on the plantation, the molasses used in the distillery, used for cooking or fed to the animals whose manure was used on the cane fields.

The hogsheads were carted from the wharf to the sugarhouse, usually not far within the major refining cities though on occasions quite some distance. Many years ago a lady from Warrington, Lancashire, recounted how as a little girl she saw raw sugar delivered to the town's sugarhouse –

From her bedroom window in a little street known as Tumber Alley she watched the carters coming in from the port of Liverpool with their loads. With old-fashioned storm lamps or flares, they came in the gloom to the Sugar House yard, sweating horses straining at the girths, whips cracking, oaths, laughter and joking, the banging and rolling of barrels, cries of "Gee-up", "Gee-back" and "Whoa, there, steady", loads taken off, "empties" taken on, and then, the transport over, by common consent an adjournment to the nearest tavern, where a tired drover might "wet his whistle" to the tune of five pints for a shilling, with a copper over for a whisp of twist and a clay pipe.[8]

Once craned up into the sugarhouse, the work of the sugar refiner began. Dodd[9] explains it very simply – *"The particles of sugar in their pure state are white; and to present them in this white crystalline form is the object of the sugar refiner"*.

The moist, dark brown muscovado would have been emptied onto the floor and then shovelled into large open-top copper cisterns set above open fires, where it was dissolved in lime water. Large quantities of bullocks' blood were added, eventually causing a scum several inches thick to form that would then be removed with a broad scraper. The scum was the albumen in the blood which when heated began to solidify collecting with it the solid impurities floating in the sugar solution. Prior to bullock's blood, eggs were used which at times were hard to come by as noted in a case in Chancery in 1690 regarding the Whitson Court Sugar House in Bristol… *"Joan [Webb] had the money and was often consulted about the Sugar House, both in the laying of pipes and the buying of eggs, 'without which the refining of sugar was impossible' …during the frosty weather of 1686 by sending out into the countryside messengers for them and paying one penny a piece for the eggs."*[10] This clarifying process may have been repeated a number of times, but then the liquor was filtered through blankets to reveal a clear reddish liquid, with further filtering only removing part of the colour which was caused by the liquor still containing small amounts of molasses.

As well as molasses, which did not crystallize, the liquor also contained water that now had to be removed by boiling, a process that also prepared the sugar itself for crystallization. The liquor was placed in a large pan over an open fire and raised to a temperature of about 240°F, sufficient to boil off the water but far too hot for the sugar and perilous for the men stirring the boiling liquid and maintaining the fires – changes would come, but not yet. Pans were usually made of conic form, five or six feet diameter at the top,

Cisterns, Useful Arts, 1846

decreasing to a diameter of about two feet six inches or three feet,[11] though the size of pan used was reduced with each successive boiling. As the water was expelled the liquor thickened and reduced in bulk to a point where it was transferred to the next pan and the process repeated. Then into the final, smallest pan where the liquor became very thick, and if allowed to cool would have granulated. The expert sugar boiler would use his experience to determine when this point was reached. A small drop of the liquor would be stretched between thumb and finger to see that it had acquired the necessary degree of consistency and granulation. The liquor would then have been removed from the fierce heat to "coolers" – pans where its temperature would have been allowed to drop to, but then maintained at, around 180°F so that granulation was still delayed.

The sugar loaf was the usual form in which the sugar was produced for sale and it was at this stage of the process that it began to take on that peculiar shape: a solid cone of anything up to around 28 inches in height – the larger the loaf, the lesser the quality. The conical moulds in which the loaves were formed were made of thick brown earthenware, open at both ends and very heavy in themselves, and when filled weighed from 25 lbs to 150 lbs. You can see the reconstructed fragments of a large one in the Southampton Museum of Archaeology, which had undoubtedly been used by John Brissault who ran the city's only sugarhouse from 1743 to his bankruptcy in 1774.[12]

In the fill house the moulds were lined up against each other in their hundreds, narrow end downwards; the small hole in that end having been plugged with paper or rag. Each mould was filled to within a few inches of the top, the very hot liquor being carried in large elongated copper basins about 1 cwt at a time from the coolers across the fill house floor to the moulds. Once in the moulds the sugar began to cool, granulate and solidify. The next day the moulds were moved to a cooler (80°F!) upper floor, the plugs removed and the small holes cleared. Each mould stood in its own earthenware jar (drip pot) so that the syrup that drained from the loaf could be collected and later re-boiled with raw sugar to produce lower grades of sugar and, once exhausted of all crystals, treacle.

After a few days the drainage was complete but there still remained small

Fill House, Useful Arts 1846

amounts of both syrup and molasses in the sugar loaves, which discoloured them. A mixture of fine white clay and water was placed onto the sugar at the top of each mould. The moisture from the wet clay filtered slowly through the sugar taking with it the remaining uncrystallized syrup and molasses. This process may have been repeated a number of times and, of course, the taller the loaf the less effective it would have been. When finished the clay was removed, the sugar flattened off and the loaves removed from their moulds. They were neatened off in a simple hand-turned rotary machine with

Turning off, Useful Arts, 1846

cutting blades forming a conical shape rather like a large pencil sharpener.

Still damp, the loaves were loaded into large ovens at about 140°F. Once thoroughly dried they were removed, cooled and then wrapped in paper, usually blue to enhance their whiteness, ready for sale to wholesalers and grocers.

The whole process took 2–3 weeks of intensive work after which all would be prepared again for the next "refine" to begin immediately. All this was overseen by the master sugar boiler, not necessarily the owner but perhaps the hired expert, and probably the only skilled man on site if the sugarhouse was a small one. He knew the exact point when the boiling sugar was ready for crystallization, he knew the time to move it from the pan to the moulds, and he ran the place in a truly autocratic manner. All the rest were labourers

and, of course, the requisite clerks to keep the orders and the accounts recorded…and I doubt that there was much change during the next two stages of the industry's development.

This is how it would have been in Christian Tielhen's time. To quote from just one double page of his Refining Book[13], a typical "refine" at his sugarhouse was the *"Twelft Refine"* (see following page). It began on 22 February 1760 and ended on 7 March yielding almost exactly 10 tons of saleable finished products. The *"Thirten Refine"* began the next day, 8 March 1760, and yielded 11 1/2 tons, such was the relentless production in the sugarhouse.

Tielhen itemised his production into 5 categories. *Loaves* would have been those of the best quality made directly from raw sugar. *Lumps* were made from a second boiling with some clear syrup added, and would not have been so fine in quality or so white in colour. *Pieces* were probably a lower grade loaf, similar to *bastards*, which were produced from the syrup that had drained from the moulds mixed with raw sugar. *Scums* were produced from the sugar extracted from the scum removed during the early clarifying and filtration processes, and from the waste from various parts of the production.

This "refine" produced over 50% best quality loaves, though we can see from his sales that these were graded by quality and the prices set accordingly. Just over 40% were his very best quality and most of these were sold directly to another refiner, Sir Thomas Rawlinson. All the lumps were sold to Bristow & Hall, perhaps a wholesaler, but the lower grade loaves were not sold in that form, having been crushed into powder. This was sold as a superior kind of moist sugar, but even this was graded by quality, the better coming from the broad part of the loaf, the poorest from the pointed end. Tielhen had a market for the molasses, and no doubt somewhere managed to sell the waste that would yield no more sugar as manure.

Nowhere in his "Refining Book" were sales totalled. Weights were recorded with great accuracy, implying that Tielhen paid duty on the weight of the products he sold rather than the revenue they produced. His

Twelft Refine…

MADE	12				SOLD	12			Price / cwt	cwt	qu	lb
1760					**1760**							
	Loaves					Loaves						
Feb 22		147			Apr 3		24	Mr Bond	82/-	2	0	5
Feb 23		154					112	Mr Bond	81/-	9	2	14
Feb 25		187	488				150	Mr Note	80/6	12	3	13
	Lumps						4	Mr Spurman	81/-	0	1	11
Feb 26		45					184	Rawlison + Co	82/-	13	3	23
Feb 27		49			Apr 25		12	Mrs Steele	81/-	1	0	6
Feb 28		46					2	Mrs Hall	81/-	0	0	15
Feb 29		46				Lumps						
Mar 1		46	232		Apr 25		232	Bristow + Hall	73/6	72	0	9
	Pieces					Molasses						
Mar 3		33	33		Apr 30			Mr Evans	15/-	9	2	10
	Bastards				Apr 28			Mr More	14/-)			
Mar 4		25			Apr 30			Mr More	14/6)	19	3	0
Mar 5		25				Ground						
Mar 6		27			May 2	– Fare		Rawlison + Co	67/-	12	1	23
Mar 7		26	103		May 2	– Middle		Mr Spalding	56/-	12	3	17
	Scums				May 2	– Tipps		Mr Spalding	47/6	40	2	16
Feb 27		1										
Mar 3		3							total	206	1	22
Mar 4		3										
Mar 5		3										
Mar 6		4										
Mar 7		4	18									

tiny "Bills Delivered Book"[14] for that period shows that he sent bills to most of his customers, sometimes over 2 months after the sales were made.

At this time the price of refined sugar was 40% greater than that of the raw sugar from which it was produced – over the next 100 years, developments in the industry would reduce that margin to 20%.[15]

For some, work began at 2 or 3 o'clock in the morning lighting fires that would heat cisterns, boil sugar, warm ovens and bring whole buildings up to their working temperature which was, by today's standards, very high indeed. Throughout the refining process ingredients and materials could catch fire at any time, and most of the interior of a sugarhouse was encrusted with sugar, deposited on floors by spillage and on everything else by the sugar-laden condensation from the pans. In Glasgow in 1725, the magistrates agreed to exempt sugarhouse servants, as the labourers were called, from keeping the town guard *"in respect their labour and work in the sugar houses nessessarilly requires their working in the night time as well as throw the day"* provided each sugarhouse boiler was prepared to have his servants attend any fire in the city immediately, taking with them the required slings, stands and buckets filled with water.[16] This was quite a sensible approach considering that amongst the most likely places for fires to occur were the sugarhouses! With such primitive fire-fighting equipment, once a fire took hold it would have been very difficult to bring under control. Chester's *Weekly Courant* reported in 1750, *"Last Monday night about 11 o'clock a fire broke out at the [Danvers] Sugar House in Liverpool which burned with such violence that in a short space of time the building was entirely consumed"*. From this time through to the late 1800s, both the national and local press carried numerous reports of sugarhouse fires, including that in February 1846 at Grant & Baldwin's, in St George's

Place, St George's in the East. The fire began in the early hours of the morning and by daybreak had totally destroyed the sugarhouse and stock valued at £20,000. The Illustrated London News reported that,

The engines were promptly on the spot, and there being an abundance of water, immense streams were continually thrown upon the burning pile: but the flames had got too firm a hold; the contents were of too inflammable a nature to admit of the slightest check, and the flames rushed rapidly from the basement, where the fire commenced, to the seven successive storeys, until the whole mass was completely encircled in one sheet of fire; and about half-past four o'clock the roof fell in with an awful crash, partially smothering the fire, but only for a moment, as it again burst forth with redoubled fury. Subsequently a great part of the east front fell, and the south wall, with the lofty chimney, was expected to fall.[17]

Sugar refining was almost a skill-less trade, but eventually the Industrial Revolution began to have an effect – the steam engine was introduced, not to provide motive power but to provide a safer method of heating and hopefully reduce the risk of fire. This was the first of two genuinely revolutionary changes made to the "old process" previously described. Heat was necessary throughout the sugarhouse and in almost every process therein, so for the steam engine to become a single source of heat was both convenient and considerably safer. Steam pipes ran to all parts of the building to provide general heat, they heated the ovens, and most importantly they boiled the sugar in the cisterns and pans. The clarifying cisterns were fitted with small pipes that forced steam up through the sugar/lime/blood mixture to heat it, giving them a new name – blow-up cisterns. The open copper pans in which the sugar was concentrated were redesigned with steam pipes attached to them so that the heat from

Fire at Grant & Baldwin, *Illustrated London News*, 28 February 1846

the steam rather than the open fires could boil the sugar. In theory, the sugar refiner was able to regulate the supply of heat to all parts and all processes as he wished. The coal and wood, along with the smoke and flames, were banished to the boiler house. Safety had been improved, though not to the extent that had been expected as, at times, it was difficult to control the steam pressure within the system.

As in other steam-powered factories, boilers did on occasions explode, and when they did there was usually loss of life. In 1816 at the sugarhouse of Mr Constadt in Well Street, St George's in the East, the new boiler holding about 2000 gallons overheated and the explosion caused a total collapse of the building killing three men including the son of Mr Spear, a partner in the concern, and injuring many more. Soon afterwards the ruins caught fire destroying the adjacent sugarhouse of the same company accounting for more lives.[18] In 1835, the boilers exploded at Ring's sugarhouse in Vauxhall Road, Liverpool, killing five men.[19] There was similar loss of life at the large refinery of Hall & Boyd in Breezers Hill, St George's in the East, in 1855 when again a boiler exploded. Frederich Mullinstedt, Johann Israel, Heinrich Frederichs and another labourer named Holstein, along with John Black, a charcoal man, all died, and Johann Henge, a stoker, was given no hope of survival.[20]

An alternative, but similar, development was Daniel Wilson's method of using oil as a heating medium. The oil was passed through pipes attached to the pans and, as it would not be near its boiling point, was much safer. This latter process required a single fire to be placed under a closed vessel containing the oil, which was then heated to 350° (its boiling point being 650°) and was then drawn off to the pans using a pump powered by the company's steam engine.

Both methods were welcomed by the fire insurance companies of the time. It had already become very expensive to insure buildings and stock because of the huge risk of fire. Refiners, initially for their own benefit, had founded the Phoenix Fire Office in order to undercut the premiums charged by the Sun Fire Office and other insurers. Once these new

processes began to be installed and proven, all the insurers drastically increased premiums for the "old process", generally charging twice the "new process" premiums, hoping to encourage change. Understandably change did not come overnight and the insurance companies found themselves introducing intermediate premiums for sugarhouses in the process of change, that had aspects of both the "old" and "new" processes operating simultaneously.

A huge fire began in the early hours of 10 November 1819 at the sugarhouse of Severn & Co (also referred to as Severn, King & Co) in Mulberry Street, off Commercial Road, London. It completely destroyed the building and led to a celebrated court case[21] which emphasized the problems of insuring "mixed" processes. The insurers, Phoenix Fire Office, who had trebled the premium, refused to pay for the loss insisting that Wilson's oil-heating process had been installed in a newly built extension to the sugarhouse without their knowledge. Severn & Co went to court in December 1820 to recover their losses and won their case. They could not only show that William Lockie, the surveyor for Phoenix, and John Cope, one of its Directors, had inspected the new process on several occasions, but called witnesses from amongst their employees and the folks who lived in the adjoining streets who had been present on the fateful night. They were unanimous in their statements that the fire had started at the far end of the building where the old pans were situated and nowhere near the part of the building which contained the oil-heating machinery. The jury found in favour of Severn & Co, awarding the full £15,000, and the judge complemented them on their verdict. Severn, King & Co made similar representation against the Imperial Insurance Co, again the insurers presented conflicting evidence, and again the jury found in the refiner's favour.[22]

The early 1800s brought improvements in both of the filtering techniques. Bag filters replaced the blanket filters used to remove the scum during clarification. A large number of long cotton cloth tubes, each closed at the bottom, were screwed to openings in the bottom of a large cistern so that they hung vertically within a tank. The sugar/lime/blood mixture was allowed into the upper cistern and flowed into the cloth tubes where the scum remained whilst the clear reddish syrup seeped through the cloth into the tank. The cloth tubes needed to be emptied and washed often, with the scum either being reprocessed in the sugarhouse or sold to a scum boiler who would boil it again and again on his own premises to remove what sugar remained. The red syrup needed to have the colour removed and at last an effective method was found – the valuable properties of charcoal were discovered. Animal charcoal, or black-bone, was produced by heating animal bones in a retort to red heat, covering them with sand, allowing them to cool and then crushing them to a coarse powder. The larger refineries often had their own retorts; otherwise a local charcoal man supplied refiners. A deep cistern was produced with a double bottom, the upper of which was pierced with numerous holes. Across this a cloth was laid, onto which animal charcoal was spread to a depth of about 3 feet and when the liquor was allowed to flow slowly in, it sank slowly through the charcoal and out below, from where a now colourless liquor was piped away to the pans. The charcoal was extremely effective at removing colour, but it had a second advantage – it could be washed and reheated repeatedly, each time regaining its original properties, and so the same batch of charcoal could be used many times over.

If the first of the "genuinely revolutionary changes", the replacing of the open fires with piped heat, was to have a great effect on working conditions and safety, the second would do that as well but would also benefit the sugar itself. The invention of the vacuum pan by the Hon Edward Charles Howard in 1813 was a masterstroke.

Howard (1774–1816) was a man of science and the younger brother of the twelfth Duke of Norfolk. He married Elizabeth, the daughter of William Maycock, a London sugar refiner,[23] and turned his attention to solving the problem of concentrating the sugar by evaporation in a way that was far less injurious to the sugar. Boiling the liquor in

open pans required a temperature of around 240°F to evaporate the water content, and although this was below the boiling point of the sugar it was realised that the quality of the sugar would improve if the liquor was boiled less fiercely. In practice, if a liquid is boiled at anything less than normal atmospheric pressure the temperature at which it boils will be proportionally lower. Howard worked to produce an apparatus that would boil the liquor at around 140°F, by creating a partial vacuum within the closed container in which the liquor boiled.

Vacuum Pan, Dodd, 1841

Dodd, in 1841,[24] described the vacuum pans at Fairrie's sugarhouse located "nearly behind Whitechapel Church" as being circular, domed, copper vessels, from six to seven feet in diameter and about the same in height, with no visible fire beneath them, as the contemporary sketch shows. The lower part of the pan was double and the bottom cavity would have been filled with steam as part of the heating process. Coiled pipes conducted more steam through the upper cavity, and thus through the liquid sugar, boiling it and evaporating the water content. The sugar, steam and evaporating water were ducted in and out of the pan, as the case maybe, by more pipe work, and there was also the all-important pump which withdrew some of the air from within the upper cavity to produce a partial vacuum. When all this came together, the liquor would boil at just over half the boiling point of water yet the water would be evaporated off because of the vacuum, but excessively high temperatures would not harm the sugar.

The vacuum pan was a very successful method of boiling sugar for crystallization, but in consequence two problems arose. Firstly, in order to determine whether the boiling was complete, the master boiler in charge needed to "touch" the sugar and draw it between finger and thumb to test its consistency. The sugar was in a closed vessel, however, and in a partial vacuum. Howard overcame this with the "proof-stick". A straight, rigid tube was fixed through the bottom cavity of the pan and into the upper cavity where the sugar boiled. The hollow proof-stick fitted tightly into this tube, and when turned opened a valve at the inner end of the tube allowing a small amount of sugar to pass into the proof-stick. When turned back again, the valve closed and the proof-stick could be withdrawn bringing with it a sample of sugar for testing without upsetting the vacuum in the pan.

When the sugar was at the correct state, the vacuum was reduced and the thick sugar was allowed to flow out, and this was where Howard met the second problem. As the sugar had only boiled at 140°F, it was already crystallizing within the vacuum pan, an undesirable situation as the brown colouring would have been contained permanently within the crystals of sugar. Rather than flow to coolers as in the earlier process, the sugar was now taken to heaters. These were open copper pans that raised the temperature to around 180°F, and with constant stirring kept the colouring matter and the sugar crystals from combining, and it was from these heaters in the fill house that the men would fill the moulds.

Howard's patent (1813) for the vacuum pan was so successful that he refused an offer of £40,000 for the patent, instead allowing refiners to use it under licence. He is said to have earned £27,000 in 1814, £40,000 in 1815 and over £60,000 in 1816, the year of his death from heat stroke following a visit to the stove room of a refinery.[25] His will[26] not only showed his concern for the well-being of his children, to whom the vast majority of his wealth and income went in trust, but it also tells us that

he benefited from a three-fifths' share of the income from his sugar patents.

By the 1840s, the vacuum pans generally contained about 100 gallons of syrup yielding around 11 cwt of sugar in each charge, though there was mention of larger ones, particularly one in a London sugarhouse that produced 18 tons of sugar loaves daily[27], nearly twice Christian Tielhen's whole "refine" back in 1760. Finzel's huge Counterslip refinery in Bristol in the 1860s and 1870s had pans capable of containing 27–30 tons of sugar each; whilst two of them – the largest in the world at the time – turned out respectively 400 and 500 tons of sugar per week.[28] I wonder if Mr Howard had ever thought that big?

So it was sugar loaves of various grades, crushed sugars, treacles and molasses that predominated production up to this time. Tons and tons of the stuff, although there was little or no nutritional justification – to quote from 1846,

> *It is curious to witness the application of so much science, ingenuity, skill, and capital; to the production of an article which, after all, is one of mere luxury, and according to Dr. Prout, is inferior in nutritive properties to the raw sugar which furnishes it, a circumstance which may afford some satisfaction to those persons whose means will not allow them to use white sugar.*[29]

There were two other products that deserve mention – spirit colour and capillaire. A by-product of the refining process, particularly on the plantations, was rum, however when distilled it was a clear liquid. "Spirit colour" was developed as a colouring for rum – a boiled dark muscovado sugar with a small amount of rum added was produced, and about 3 pints would colour 100 gallons of spirit.[30] Today a whole trade has developed with our greater "need" for food and drink colourings, many still based on sugar. "Capillaire" was a water-clear syrup originally flavoured with dried maidenhair fern though later with orange-flower water, much used by confectioners as a flavouring, and also as a cordial.[31] Either side of 1800, the sale of capillaire as a refreshment was often mentioned in the advertisements on the front of *The Times*. The small number of refiners who manufactured these products often styled themselves as *"Liquid Refined Sugar Makers"*, and used stoneware flagons in which to sell their syrups, assumedly on a sale-or-return basis.

Charles Smith (1806–1873) was brought up in the trade. He worked for his father, John Smith, before taking over the family business at 50 Upper Thames Street, London, in 1832 following his father's death. He was soon trading as "capillaire maker and spirit colour manufacturer" though was listed personally in the Pigot's 1836 Directory as "sugar refiner". He moved both family and business to 203 Upper Thames Street in 1837, and in 1840 went into partnership with Robert Tyers under the name of Smith & Tyers Liquid Sugar Refiners, before moving to 14 Green Street, Blackfriars Road, Southwark, in 1853. The flagon shown can be dated to 1837–9, as Smith & Tyers used flagons showing that company name though still at 203 Upper Thames Street.

We see few of these products today, although molasses and dark treacles are used in cooking. Small sugar loaves are still made in parts of continental Europe especially for Feuerzangenbowle, a winter punch which involves soaking a sugar loaf with rum and setting it alight so that it caramelises and drips into a hot spiced red wine and fruit mixture. Granulated sugar and, to a lesser extent, cube sugar are our common varieties. Centrifugal machines, invented for drying dyed wool and cloth, were put to use in larger refineries for drying filter bags, etc, and in the second half of the 19th century the opportunity was seen to use them for separating the sugar crystals from the remaining colouring matter instead of making sugar loaves in moulds. With the sugar from the vacuum pan inside a rapidly spinning drum, the colouring matter and any remaining moisture was forced out through the finely perforated walls of the drum leaving the clean, dry sugar crystals trapped within.

The picture shows the crystals being mixed at the Counterslip Refinery, Bristol, in 1873, where each centrifugal machine, and there were many on the two floors above, produced the finished sugar at a rate of $1^{1}/_{2}$ cwt in $1^{1}/_{2}$ minutes. Mixing, using wooden shovels, was necessary as the size of the crystals varied depending upon where they formed in the mass of liquid sugar in the pans.

 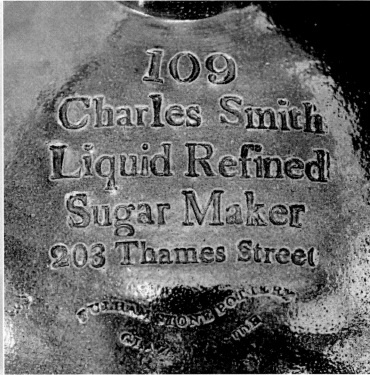

6 gallon flagon, Charles Smith, c1838, © Bryan Mawer

Counterslip Refinery, Bristol, *Illustrated London News*, 29 November 1873

Gravity moved the sugar once again, as it was bagged on the floor below.[32]

There had been various attempts to produce sugar cubes on a large scale, it being thought necessary to replace the weight and inconvenience of the sugar loaf with something smaller, making it more suitable to both the grocer and the householder. In 1875, Henry Tate, jointly with David Martineau & Sons, purchased the rights to use the Langen process for producing sugar cubes, and it was this decision that would make the difference between success and failure for his new Thames Refinery at Silvertown. Needless to say, the German process was used successfully until 1894 when Tate purchased the rights to the Belgian process invented by Adant, which would continue in use until 1961.[33]

It would be wrong not to mention one absolutely essential trade which had nothing to do with the processing of sugar – that of the cooper. Raw sugar arrived from overseas in wooden barrels and hogsheads (even larger barrels) that because of the nature of their sticky contents had to be broken open in order to empty them, and some forms of sugar were sold to wholesalers and grocers in barrels. All these barrels had to be made from either new materials or from the wreckage of the broken ones, leading to coopers setting up in business close to refineries. With many of London's refiners in the Upper Thames Street area of the

City in the second half of the 18th century, many coopers, and indeed the brokers who bought and sold the sugar, set up businesses conveniently close in the lanes around Lower Thames Street and Gt Tower Street, just west of the Tower. For example, Woodhouse in Cross Lane, Eustace in Water Lane and Humfrey & Man in Harp Lane. Once into the 19th century though, many large refineries had their own cooperages and employed their own coopers, leading to the distinct occupation of "sugar cooper" often found in later censuses.

Neither should we forget the clerks working at the sugarhouses. No doubt everything had to be recorded as the taxes of the day had to be paid for all sorts of reasons on raw sugar through to the finished products. Parliament passed acts regarding sugar with such frequency it is a wonder the changes could be kept up with – acts imposing or suspending duty on imports, and bounties on exports for each and every different type of sugar as well as the packages they were shipped in. At Cuppins Lane, Chester, Nathaniel Bishop, the clerk to the business, negotiated a new arrangement in 1767 whereby he was to be paid £84 pa + 1/16th share of the clear profits. The productivity bonus was not forthcoming, however, and in 1773 he demanded the £2538 16s 3d he was owed.[34] Charles Bishry was another such clerk; born in Alie Street in 1830, he died in the Mile End Workhouse aged 52. He is listed as a sugar refiner's clerk in the four censuses from 1851, and as he married Caroline Priggen, a daughter of refiner Jacob Priggen, in 1854, it is probable that for some time at least he worked at Priggen's sugarhouse at 35 Gloucester Street.

The politeness of the times belied the harshness of the working environment. A sugar refiner applying for a situation around 1870 was advised to use a Victorian sample letter of application[35] that read,

Gentlemen,
Being out of employment at present, and hearing you required a sober, steady, active, and pushing man to superintend your business upstairs, I

*write to inform you that for years I was head
upstairs man at Messrs. – and Co. You will see
by the enclosed copy of a testimonial from them
that the duties of filling out the goods up to the
stoving, were carried out in such a manner as to
convince them I thoroughly understood the
business. A reply at your convenience will much
oblige,*
Yours respectfully,

Now that applicant would have known what
he was getting himself into, but to an out-of-
work agricultural worker from the cold,
windswept north of Germany to whom city
life was probably unknown, the prospect of a
warm indoor job with accommodation and
meals provided, and as much free beer as he
could drink, albeit in a different country,
would have sounded very attractive. Those
who told him of the opportunities in London
or Liverpool were hardly likely to mention
that the work would be extremely hot,
exhausting and dangerous, the hours very
long indeed, breathing an atmosphere laden
with hot sugar vapour, and that all workers
were continually exposed to the risks from
boiling sugar, scorching containers, scalding
steam, unsavoury substances, heavy objects,
poor building design and, of course, fire.

Fire would always be a threat to buildings
and stock (there were over 30 major East End
refinery fires between 1800 and 1847) but these
were heavily insured, whereas the workers'
safety was a different matter.

- 1879 Sep 15, Hans Rathgen, age 69,
  sugarbaker. Cause of death – shock to the
  system from scalds through having fallen
  into a pan of boiling sugar. Accidental.
  Middlesex Coroner's inquest held 18 Sept
  1879.
- 1877 Nov 27, Jacob Gramlich died in an
  accident at work in a Sugar House at 15
  Christian Street, St George's in the East.
  Following an inquest, his death certificate
  read, "Labourer at a sugar refinery –
  violent – contused brain – crushed in a lift
  accidentally".

Whether anything was learnt from these
accidents, and conditions improved, is
doubtful. Some 60 years earlier there was a
general lack of concern and responsibility as
exposed by a series of Coroners' Inquests[36] in
the Whitechapel area around 1820, where the
Coroners refused to place any blame upon the
refineries by not naming them and simply
using the phrase "*... in a certain sugarhouse in
the said parish...* ", or upon the management by
placing the responsibility on the workers by
using the phrase "*... accidentally, casually and
by misfortune...* ".

By a huge coincidence, the Foreman of the
Jurors for the Inquest on 20 January 1820 of
the unfortunate John Connor was my 3xgt
grandfather Henry Almeroth, age 25, grocer of
Whitechapel.

> *That on the eleventh day of December
> [1819]... the said John Connor being at work in
> a certain sugarhouse it so happened accidentally
> casually and by misfortune that one of the
> ceilings of the said sugarhouse gave way and fell
> upon him... he did receive mortal bruises and
> fractures on the head and body... he did languish
> and live in the parish from [that day] until the
> eighteenth of January [1820]... when he did
> die... the jurors do say that he accidentally came
> to his death and not otherwise.*

There are other inquests in that same series
with very similar wording, both inside the
sugarhouse –

- 1820 Aug 24, Carsten Schroder – "Fell
  through pulley hole to ground... St
  George's in the East". Accidental death.
- 1821 Jan 29, Frederick Sauer – "Fell
  through loop hole of sugarhouse to
  ground... Whitechapel". Accidental death.
- 1821 Apr 6, Christopher Filling – "Fell
  through pulley hole in sugarhouse...
  Shadwell". Accidental death.
- 1822 Aug 14, John Cope – "Pot fell on
  head while working in sugarhouse...
  Whitechapel... died instantly..."
  Accidental death.
- 1828, Henry William Lutgen – "Fell into
  scum boiler in scum warehouse...
  Whitechapel". Accidental death.

– And outside the sugarhouse –

- 1820 Sep 20, John Beck – "Struck on leg by cask of sugar… at West India Dock, Whitechapel". Accidental death.
- 1820 Oct 10, Henry Eckworth – "Case of sugar fell on him from a truck… at London Docks, Whitechapel". Accidental death.
- 1821 May 21, George Bryant – "Cask of sugar rolled on his leg… at Poplar…" Accidental death.

Reports of accidents and inquests usually appeared in the local, and often national, press. Collections were taken for the families of the dead and injured after such accidents, and the odd few pennies may have appeared from a charity or two, but there was no state fund to help out, nor was there any form of compensation. The London Hospital was close to the East End sugarhouses when an accident did happen, and no doubt the other major centres had local hospitals that were well used.

This was not an occupation for the faint-hearted; many died young, but some lived on into their 70s and 80s, though "retirement" was rarely a possibility for the labourers, only for the owners. Perhaps the older workers would have been rewarded with less strenuous work in the sugarhouse until illness or the rigours of the job got the better of them. We have to hope that good work and years of loyal service were recognized as in the case of Claus Heinrich Schuhmacher (1824–92), a Hanoverian sugarbaker, who had worked for Grant & Baldwin from their re-opening after their refinery fire in 1846, through until 1852. He left with a testimonial from his employers, which appears to have stood him in good stead for the future.

He journeyed to the West Indies where he worked for 3 years, before returning to take up the post of sugar boiler at the newly built Sankey Sugar Works at Earlestown in Lancashire, which opened in 1855. He lived in one of the larger cottages (no 11) provided for the workers, this one being right next to the refinery buildings, and by 1881 was listed as foreman. He retired with a company pension in 1889, and was buried in Earlestown Cemetery in 1892.

For some it was a job that lasted a few years, just until they got settled in a neighbourhood and managed to find something less arduous, whilst for others it was until they had saved enough money for that journey to North America, or to return to Germany or Poland. Many stuck at it hoping an opportunity would arise, and in some cases it did. Horst Rössler[37] writes,

It is known from other trades that drinking by occupation in particular pubs was common. It is highly probable that the sugarbakers also favoured certain pubs particularly so since a good many of the Hanoverian immigrants after some years of working in the sugar refineries set up for themselves and became publicans. These

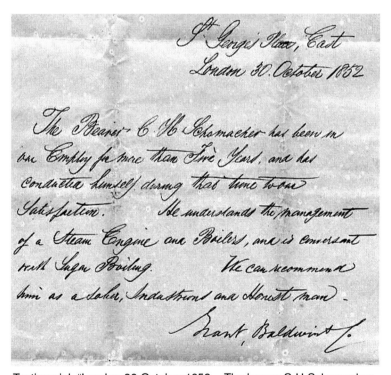

Testimonial, "London 30 October 1852 – The bearer C H Schumacher has been in our employ for more than five years, and has conducted himself during that time to our satisfaction. He understands the management of a steam engine and boilers, and is conversant with sugar boiling. We can recommend him as a sober, industrious and honest man. – Grant, Baldwin & Co.", © David Parr *public houses run by former sugarbakers must have been relevant institutions in the community of immigrant sugarbakers. They were news and information centres...*

Johann Bullwinkel (1820–1874) arrived in London aged 18 and is shown working for Hall & Boyd in Breezers Hill, St George's in the East, in the 1841 and 1851 censuses. He ran the Red Lion at 196/7 St George's Street, directly opposite Hall & Boyd, from at least 1861 until his death.

Hinrich Intermann was the publican at the Crown at 14 Rupert Street, next door to the refinery of C R & R Dames, from at least 1867. The German language weekly "Hermann" recommended this public house "for its good food and drink as well as musical presentations 3 evenings in the week".[38] Intermann was a German sugar boiler living with his family at 8 Rupert Street, Whitechapel in 1861, and probably working at Dames' or either of the other two sugarhouses in that street, before taking over the Crown from Sarah Betjemann, widow of another former sugarbaker, Hinrich Betjemann. Similarly, Balthasar Heuser was a London sugarbaker for at least the nine years following his marriage in 1856. By 1865 he was living, and probably working, in Christian Street, and the 1871 census shows him as the landlord of the Beehive at 71 Christian Street.

Stephen Shilling married in London in 1791 but moved to Hull and worked as a sugarbaker, and later as "confidential servant", at Thornton, Watson & Co, sugar refiners, through until about 1814. After a short time as a grocer he became the landlord of the Three Crowns, Lime Street, just up the road from the sugarhouse. He died in 1829 aged 62.

So it was beer throughout the working day, beer in the evening, and they had Sundays off for church, rest... and a beer.

Seriously though, sugar refining was not a pleasant job, and we have to hope that most enjoyed their work, but I think I can see why Herman Almeroth's sons did not follow him into the trade!

Notes

1   *Diseases in London*, R. Willan, 1800 (Phoenix Assurance & the development of British Insurance, Vol 1, C. Trebilcock, CUP, 1985).

2   "A Day at a Sugar Refinery" by G. Dodd, *The Penny Magazine*, no. 582, April 1841.

3   *The History of Sugar* by Noel Deerr, Chapman & Hall, 1950.

4   *Sugar – The Grass that changed the World* by Sanjida O'Connell, Virgin Books, 2004.

5   Deerr (note 3).

6   O'Connell (note 4).

7   *Cane Sugar* by Noel Deerr, Norman Rodger 1921.

8   "Sugar Refining – another of Warrington's lost trades", *Warrington Guardian* 7 November 1936.

9   Dodd (note 2).

10 Bristol Record Office 36772 box 5.

11 Chambers *Cyclopaedia: or, an Universal Dictionary of Arts and Sciences*, 1783.

12 *Sugar Refining in Southampton* by J.C. Drake, Southampton Museum of Archaeology.

13 The National Archives C104/211.

14 The National Archives C104/211.

15 *The Useful Arts & Manufactures of Gt Britain – Sugar*, Soc of Promoting Christian Knowledge, 1846.

16 Extract from the Minutes of The Burgh of Glasgow, 11th December 1725, via; *Proud Record, The Story of the Glasgow Fire Service*, Campbell Steven, 1975.

17 *The Illustrated London News*, 28 February 1846, p 148.

18 AGFHS Sugarbakers Guide, 1st edition.

19 *The Times*, May 1835.

20 *The Times*, 16 November 1855.

21 Cambridge University Library – PX1282–4. (Verbatim account in three handwritten volumes, each some 250 pages).

22 Deerr (note 3).

23 Deerr (note 3).

24 Dodd (note 2).

25 "The Life and Work of Edward Charles Howard FRP" by Frederick Kurzer, in *Annals of Science, 56 (2)*, April 1999.

26 The National Archives PROB 11/1587.

27 Useful Arts (note 15).

28 *The Illustrated London News*, 29 November 1873, p 515.

29 Useful Arts (note 15).

30 *Sugar – A Handbook for Planters & Refiners* by Lock & Newlands Bros, pub Spon 1888.

31 Lock & Newlands (note 30).

32 *The Illustrated London News* (note 28).

33 *Sugar & All That* by Antony Hugill, Gentry Books, 1978.

34 Cheshire and Chester Archives & Local Studies CCALS D/HINCKS/66.

35 *The Ladies' and Gentleman's Model Letter Writer*, c1870.

36 London Metropolitan Archives – MJ/SPC/E/~.

37 "Germans in the British Sugar Industry: Work, Culture, Religion", Horst Rössler, lecture at Greenwich, July 2004.

38 *Hermann* (3 August 1867), from Horst Rössler.

THE SMELL

"A gust of wind brings the thick spicy smell of molasses liquor from Tate's. Jenny loves that overpowering Silvertown smell, the sheer weight and history of sugar."

Silvertown, by Melanie McGrath, Fourth Estate, 2002. ISBN 1 84115 142 4

Appendix 1
Sugarhouse Fires

(collected so far)

1749	Sugarhouse in Angel Alley, Church Lane, Whitechapel.
1750	Danvers, Liverpool.
1783 Nov 20	King Street Sugarhouse, Glasgow.
1791 Dec 13	Mr Engell's sugar factory, Wellclose Square.
1792 Oct 5	Mr Phillips sugar factory, Glasgow.
1793	Hunter, Robinson, Wilson, Ritchie, Ramsey, MacCann & Macfie, Greenock.
1793/4	William Coslett, Church Lane, Whitechapel.
1795	Hunter, Robinson, Wilson, Ritchie, Ramsey, MacCann & Macfie, Greenock.
1797	Messrs Coope & Co, Osborne Street, Whitechapel.
<1799	Fisher, East Smithfield.
1799 Apr 29	Messrs Chambers sugar factory, Gloucester.
1800 Feb 1	Messrs Friecke & Endelman's sugar factory, Thames Street.
1800 Oct 2	Messrs Atherton, Davis & Toundras sugar factory, Liverpool.
<1801	Grobb, Thames Street.
1816	Constadt & Spear, Well Street, Wellclose Square.
1819 Jul 29	Messrs Craven & sugar factory, Nelson Street, Whitechapel.
1819 Nov 10	Messrs Severn & King sugar factory, Church Lane, Whitechapel.
1820	Ryder & Nasmyth, (Old Gravel Lane?).
1820 Oct 23	At sugarbakers in Old Gravel Lane – great loss of life.
1821 Apr 6	Messrs Burnell & Gies, Church Street, Mile End New Town.
1822 Jan 28	Messrs Rohde & Co sugar factory, Leman Street.
1822	Wm Macfie & Co, Elbe Street, Leith.
1824	Mr Alderman Lucas, Osborne Street, Whitechapel.
1826 Dec 27	Ledlard's sugar factory, Bristol.
1827 Apr 25	Soulie, Jones & Co sugar factory, Bordeaux.
1829 Jan 12	Webb's sugar refinery, Oldham Street, Liverpool.
1829	Banks, Old Fish Street.
1829 Jan 22	Guppy's sugar refinery, Bristol.
1829 Jun 4	Friend & Boden's sugar factory, Charlotte Street, Commercial Road.
1829 Apr 22	Wm Macfie & Co, Elbe Street, Leith.
1830	Sugarhouse on the corner of Mansell Street, in Goodman's Yard.
1830	Carsten Holthouse's sugarhouse, Back Lane, St George's in the East.
1831 Apr 1	Mr Farmer's sugarhouse, Osborne Street, Whitechapel.
1831 Aug 4	Smith's sugarhouse, Dock Street, Rosemary Lane.
1832 May 26	George & Harwood's sugar factory, Lower Thames Street.
1833 Jan 4	Bowman's sugarhouse, Gowers Walk, Whitechapel.
1833 Feb 16	Wilde's sugar factory, High Street, St Lukes.
1834	Mr Banks, Osborne Street, Whitechapel.

1834 Sep 13	Watson's sugarhouse, Ratcliffe Cross.
1835 May 14	Explosion of boilers at Ring's sugarhouse in Vauxhall Road, Liverpool – 5 dead.
1836	Clayton & Thomas sugar refinery, Lower Deptford.
1836 Mar 30	Miller's sugar warehouse, Hackins Way.
1836 Jul 4	Mr Beriot's sugar works, Lille.
1838 Feb 8	Messrs Licht & Cos, Pest, Hungary.
1838 Aug 11	Messrs Petiots, Les Alouettes.
1838 Nov 27	Mr Zabell, Dunk Street / King Edward Street, MENT (uninsured).
1838	Francis Bowman & Son, Duncan Street.
1840 Dec 28	Goodhart's sugar factory, Ratcliffe Highway.
1841	Speirs & Wrede, Greenock.
1842	Cope, London.
1843 Dec 29	Martineau's sugar refinery, Goulston Street.
1843 Dec 29	Branker's sugar refinery, Liverpool.
1844 Jun 17	Craven & Lucas sugar refinery, Whitechapel.
1846 Feb	Grant & Baldwin, 17$\frac{1}{2}$ St George's Place, Back Road, St George's in the East.
1846	James Fairrie & Co, Greenock.
1846 Sep 21	Branker's sugar works, Liverpool.
1847	Connal & Parker, Greenock.
1847 Aug 26	Craven's sugar refinery, Whitechapel.
1848 Jul	Matthew Parker, Greenock.
1848 Nov	Wilson & Sons, Alston Street, Glasgow.
1849 (abt)	James Watson, Alston Street, Glasgow.
1849	Wainwright & Co, Washington Street, Glasgow.
1851	Alexander & Thomas Anderson, Greenock.
1855	Hall & Boyd, St George's in the East. Boiler explosion – 6 dead.
1857 Mar 8	Wm & James Ferguson, Greenock.
1859 Feb	Duncan's, Greenock.
1861 Mar	Crawhall, Shultz & Co, Greenock.
1861 Jun	Walker's, Greenock.
1863 Jun 24	Walker's, Greenock.
1864 Mar 22	Crawhall, Shultz & Co, Greenock.
1865 Jan 23	Murdoch & Doddrell, Port Dundas, Glasgow.
1865 Oct 18	Neill, Dempster & Neill, Greenock.
1866 Dec 17	Deer Park Sugar Refinery, Greenock.
1867 Dec 23	Blair, Reid & Steele, Greenock.
1868 Aug 14	Paul, Sword & Co, Greenock.
1868 Aug 19	Orchard's, Greenock.
1872 Jun 18	A Anderson & Sons, Greenock.
1873	P Kuck, Christian Street.
1873 Feb 25	John Walker & Co, Greenock.
1876 Nov 14	Blair, Reid & Steele, Greenock.
1877 Nov 19	Anderson's Cappielow Sugar Refinery, Greenock.
1880 Jan 6	MacEachran's, Greenock.
1882 Jan 6	MacEachran's, Greenock.
1894 Oct 30	Garston Sugar Refinery, Liverpool – large explosion.
1895 Oct 3	Glebe, Greenock.

Appendix 2
Sugarhouse Advertisements

(one per decade)

1787

To be Sold, the WEST SUGAR HOUSE Buildings, Glasgow, having a front of 104 feet to the Candleriggs-street, and 126 feet to Bell's Wynd-street. The grounds are well situated for building shops and warehouses on. Until the subjects are sold, the business will be carried on as usual. There are at present for sale, all kinds of refined Sugars, Powders, Molasses, &c. &c. For particulars apply to Alexander Scheviz.
(*The Glasgow Mercury*, 15 August 1787)

1793

By Mr Winstanley, on the premises at PAUL'S WHARF, Upper Thames Street, London, on Thursday 14 inst at 11 o'clock…
The valuable plant, utensils and fixtures of a 5-pan sugarhouse consisting of 5 large copper pans, 3 coolers, 1 refining cistern, 4 large cisterns lined with lead, abt 250 ft of copper, lead and pewter pipe, 2 iron cockles with 90 ft of pipe, 11 iron doors, 1600 pots and moulds, copper pumps, basins, ladles, lime clay mould and water cisterns, a large and very complete sugar mill with iron roll, capital scale beam and planks, 50 cwt of iron weights, an iron crane, together with a complete assortment of utensils in the sugar refining branch, brewing vessels, and other articles. The whole in very good condition having been new within 3 yrs. The same day will be sold the remaining years of the lease of a capacious five pan sugarhouse adjoining the above, with a roomy convenient dwelling house. The plant, fixtures and utensils of which are to be taken by appraisement.
(*The Times*, 7 February 1793)

1806

To be sold at Garraway's Coffee House, Change Alley, London, on 8 August…
a) Newly erected 3-pan sugarhouse in BROKEN WHARF, Upper Thames Street, consisting : 6 working floors, warehouse, storerooms, drying rooms, fillhouse, mill house, ware rooms over, dwelling house with 4 bedrooms, 2 parlours, etc, accompanying house with sample rooms, men's kitchen, brick dwelling house adjoining (being 48 Upper Thames Street) currently let.
b) Another at 44 UPPER THAMES ST, newly built, consisting : 7 working floors, about 7 ft each, large lofts, warehouse, lump room, spacious lofty light fillhouse, stove, coal cellar, mill room, 2 warehouses, yard etc, dwelling house.
(Papers of the Fishmonger's Company at TNA C217/61)

1817–19

26.4.1817 and 17.1.1818 – Following the bankruptcy of John Boyes the elder.
Sculcoates Sugar House, generally known as The New Sugar House.
A capital well-built 3 pan sugarhouse at Sculcoates adjoining the Port of Hull, and in the late occupation of Messrs. G F Boyes & Co together with plant apparatus and utensils, in excellent condition. Comprising on the

basement, a boiling house, scum house, mill house, mill warehouse, brew house and arched cellar; on the first floor an excellent counting house and warehouses; with seven other floors. Also a good substantial family dwelling house adjoining, containing dining and drawing rooms, suitable lodging rooms, kitchen, offices and fronting onto a handsome lawn and fruitful garden. Also 3 tenements for workmen and a three-stall stable and hayloft. Freehold, its front on the south of Church Street is 148 ft, its front onto the River Hull is 170 ft, well enclosed. The purchaser has the option of taking the pans, coolers, cisterns and all other fixtures and utensils at a fair appraisement. Deserving of attention as there is only one other sugarhouse in the Port of Hull.
13.2.1819 – To be sold by auction – By order of the administrator of the late Miss Harrison. All the moveable utensils etc of the New Sugar House, Hull, comprising 3 large copper pans, a horse mill and pump, about 2 tons of blue, brown and white paper; a small fire engine, a great number of tools, moulds, jars etc.
(*Hull Advertiser & Exchange Gazette*)

1823

By Mr Ellis at Garraway's on Tuesday 18 March, by the direction of the executor of George Dettmar deceased…
The whole of the extensive freehold premises situate on the west side of OSBORN ST, Whitechapel, London, in the occupation of Messrs Dettmar & Son sugar refiners. A 3 pan sugarhouse of 7 floors, a 2 pan sugarhouse of 7 floors, a 1 pan sugarhouse of 6 floors, a 2 pan scum house, counting house, dwelling house for men, brewhouse, and yard enclosed by gates. A capital residence, coach house, 4-stall stable and yard. The whole of the premises are freehold and in excellent repair.
(*The Times*, 23 March 1823)

1837

By Mr Fuller on the premises of 10 BETTS ST, Ratcliff Highway, London, on Thursday 14 September at 12 o'clock…
The plant of a patent sugar refinery, nearly new: including a large vacuum pan and heater of the most improved construction, copper blowing-up cistern, worm, pneumatic pan, filter, circular copper cistern, set vacuum pumps, high pressure steam engine and boiler, wrought iron wagon, steam boiler of 4 horsepower, Fawcett's patent steam condenser, copper and lead pipe, 2 large lead molasses cisterns, pulling-up engine, 20 iron doors, the fittings of a stove, 2 large wrought iron cisterns, a patent bottle washing machine, 10 gross of bottles, house fixtures, etc. At the same time to be sold: a newly-built brick dwelling house unfinished adjoining the sugarhouse, and a large yard enclosed with folding gates. Held for an unexpired term of 50 yrs, subject to a ground rent of £6 per annum.
(*The Times*, 9 September 1837)

1840

By Mr Fuller on the premises on the corner of RUPERT ST and GT ALIE ST, London, on Monday June 29 at 11 o'clock…
The plant, machinery and utensils of a sugar refinery; a six foot vacuum pan, melting pan, vacuum pump, open copper boiling pan, 2 coolers, blowing-up cistern, liquor cistern, filter fitted with caps and rings, copper molasses cistern, 2 horsepower high pressure steam engine, Fawcett's patent cast iron cylindrical steam boiler, in compartments 21 ft long, a wrought iron boiler, a pulling-up machine, capital single purchase crane, hogshead trucks, hogshead steamer, oak cisterns, 10,000 pots and moulds, 2 town carts, grocery utensils, coffee roasting machine, sugar crushing machine, copper scales and weights, truck, japanned canisters, and the remaining stock in trade, counting house and house fixtures, etc.
(*The Times*, 10 June 1840)

1853

By Messrs Fuller & Horsey on the premises at STRATFORD, Essex, near Bow Bridge, and on the banks of the River Lea, on Monday November 7 at 11…
The plant and utensils of a sugar refinery: large copper vacuum pan, 6 copper heaters in iron cases 6 ft diameter, 3 copper cisterns, 11 wrought iron charcoal filters (4 by Fraser), 6 square bag filters with 72 bells in each and receivers, range of bag filters with 150 bells, wrought iron blowing-up cistern lined with lead, 20 wrought iron liquor and syrup cisterns, brass force pumps, 10 horsepower high pressure steam engine with vacuum pump, set liquor pumps with pipes and cocks, 5 large cast iron tanks in plates, lead cisterns, wrought iron mould cisterns, 2 wrought iron steam boilers 15 and 30 ft long, 4 cast iron pans lined with lead, 3 lead pans in iron-bound cases, wrought iron hogshead steamer, hydraulic press with 9 in ram and press, sugar mill with knives and case, sugar crushing mill, scales and weights, weighing machine, large lead treacle cistern, the racks and fitting in stove, 4 charcoal retorts with brickwork, 2 pairs of gassing pumps, pair of testing scales, Finzel's centrifugal pan, fittings in counting house and men's room, beds and bedding, 2,000 wrought iron moulds, 2,000 earthen pots, and numerous other effects. At the same time will be sold the lease of the Sugar Refinery, with wharf and yard, held for a term of years for a very low rent.
(*The Times*, 27 October 1853)

1866

i. Failure through bankruptcy of Messrs Fincken & Co, sugar refiners, of St Phillip's Marsh, a comparatively new firm of only a few years. Liabilities of £16,000, plant etc will cover it.
ii. Auction… 7 steam engines, 4 boilers, 9 centrifugal machines, 3 vacuum pans, 10 charcoal cisterns, steam box, water tanks, 1000 bastard moulds, pug mills and shafting, steam and water pipes, valves and cocks throughout, charcoal wagons and carts, lathes, tools, other

articles. Buildings and machinery nearly new, £10,000. Lease 28 yrs at rent of £200 pa of which £80 is underlet to tenants. 110 tons of refiners charcoal. Small outlay would enable works to turn out 100 tons per week. Premises are waterside and newly erected.
(*Bristol Times & Mirror*, 21 April 1866 & 4 August 1866 at BRO 36772 Box 7)

1870

By Messrs Fuller, Horsey, Son & Co…
Lot 1… A substantial brick built sugar house, fronting PENNINGTON ST, London, with loophole doors, having 7 floors including the fill house, and a second sugar house of 9 floors, 2 stoves, steam engine house, 2 boiler houses, a building adjoining, a lofty brick built circular chimney shaft, 3 dwelling houses (nos. 2, 3, 4 St George's Street), sheds, and large open yard with entrance gates. Occupies 20,000 feet. The sugar houses are fitted with modern and appropriate plant and machinery calculated to produce about 100 tons of refined goods per week, including a copper jacketed vacuum pan 7 ft diameter 4 ft 8 in deep, 4 copper heaters, 28 copper, lead-lined and wrought iron syrup and liquor cisterns, 5 blow-up cisterns with copper worms, 6 filters with gun metal bells, 7 charcoal cisterns, 2 pairs of Manlove & Allott centrifugal machines, syrup and lift pumps, steam crane and pulling up machine, sugar shaving machine, 2 hogshead steamers, a 25 horsepower condensing steam engine, a horizontal steam engine, 4 double and single flue Cornish boilers, egg-end boiler, hydraulic scum press, fittings, pipes, pots and moulds and the necessary utensils.
(*The Times*, 22 January 1870)

1881

Renfrewshire… Blair, Reid & Steele Ltd in liquidation…
To be sold by public roup within the Faculty Hall, St George's Place, Glasgow on Wednesday 2 Nov 1881 at 1 o'clock, unless previously disposed of by private bargain,

Ingleston Sugar Refinery, Greenock, together with the goodwill of the business and all the plant, machinery, and utensils, the property of the vendors, situate therein. The sugar house is situate on the SHAWS WATER AQUEDUCT and is capable of refining 600 tons of raw sugar per week. The ground occupied by the house extends to 11,000 sq yards on which there is no feu duty. Adjoining are the office, manager's house, laboratory, on which there is a small feu duty. Upset price to ensure competition £27,500. The stock of charcoal, about 800 tons, which is all in excellent working condition, will require to be taken over by the purchaser at a valuation.
(*The Times*, 17 October 1881)

1892

Messrs Fuller, Horsey, Sons & Cassell are instructed by Messrs David Martineau & Sons Ltd (who are concentrating their business Clyde Wharf, Victoria Docks, London) to sell by auction in lots on the premises at 6 CHRISTIAN ST, London, on Tuesday 12 July 1892 at noon…
The surplus plant and machinery including 2 copper vacuum pans with condensers, 8 blow-up cisterns, 21 centrifugal machines, elevator, tramways, 5 pug mills, 22 bag filters, 3 scum filters, 4 receivers, 69 cisterns and tanks, copper refrigerator, water-softening apparatus, loaf-sugar pressing machine, montejus filter press and air pump, 2 agitating tanks, Kortling's blower, 5 steam lifts and hoists, 10 lead lined cisterns, sulphur plant, 8 charcoal reburning kilns, 20 charcoal wagons, 29 charcoal cisterns, 5 Wilson's gas producers, 4 Lancashire boilers, 2 Root's water-tube boilers, 2 pumping engines, 20 horsepower beam engine and pair of vacuum pumps, 10 horsepower beam engine and pair of gun metal air pumps, 16 horsepower horizontal engine, 2 auxiliary beams and pair of vacuum pumps, pair horizontal engines, 4 other engines, 5 gun metal pumps, iron bridge, the iron fittings of 6 drying stoves, 10 ton Hart's weighbridge, 18,000 iron moulds, etc.
(*The Times*, 9 July 1892)

1909

By Messrs Fuller, Horsey, Sons & Cassell on 20 April 1909…
Lot 1… Freehold lands and buildings at Bristol, situate in [OLD] MARKET ST with frontage thereto 167 ft, parallel frontage to Jacob Street 198 ft, nearly rectangular ground area about 4,130 sq yds. Lately in the occupation of The Bristol Sugar Refinery. The property is centrally situate, and the buildings are adaptable to other trade purposes. Independent and abundant supply of water.
Lot 2… Freehold warehouse and land in Unity Street with frontage thereto 131 ft, frontage to Jacob Street 167 ft, total area 2,770 sq yds. The buildings include very substantial brick built sugar warehouse, boiler house, chimney shaft, and 2 rows of cottages. Both lots to be sold with possession.
… And the sugar refining plant and machinery at [Old] Market Street, Bristol, including 5 copper vacuum pans, air and vacuum pumps, copper melting pans, copper steel and iron tanks, copper boiling pans, receivers, shoots, several miles of copper lead steel and other piping, water softening and purifying apparatus, blow up cisterns, bag filters, gun metal pumps, hydraulic pumps and presses, sugar mixers, Newhall's sugar dryer, bench of five 48 in Watson & Laidlaw turbine driven hydro extractors, 5 steam driven hydro extractors, iron charcoal cisterns, kilns and coolers, disintegrators, hoists, lifts and cranes, elevators and conveyors, millwright's tools, lathes, saw benches, steam engines, Lancashire boilers, economizers, Worthington, deep-well and other pumps, several hundred tons of plates, etc.
(*The Times*, 20 March 1909)

Appendix 3
Directory of Sugar Refineries

London; Bristol – Whitehaven.

(Sources searched so far indicate that these people ran refineries for the dates shown, however this may not represent the full extent of their time at the premises.)

LONDON

CITY

BISHOP'S CT, OLD BAILEY

1727 FELLOWS, T
1761 DAVIS & BEST
1762 DAVIS, BEST & SCHULERMAN
1789–93 KELLER Philip
1791 WILZ Mary
1794 WITTE Henry
1797–8 SEDGEWICK & SPRADO
1811–17 COATES Thomas
1811–17 FRIEAKE & CREED

BREAD STREET HILL

1729 LEWIS, E
1732–4 HORTON & IDLE
1735–41, 44, 49, 60 HORTON, J
1741 COAPE & COE
1759–66 BAAS Joachim Gerrard
1761–3 BASS & HAMMOND
1768–72 DEICHMAN George (no 21)
1772 BASS Joachim Gechard
1777–8 STRICKLAND & GRIFFIN
1780 MILLER & SAMLER (no 21)
1783 STRICKLAND William (no 16)
1786 TOWGOOD, DANVERS & VOGLE
1789–90s STRICKLAND William (no 16)
1790–1817 TOWGOOD, DANVERS & Co (no 21)
1791–1818 TOWGOOD, DANVERS & CERIAKES
1817 DANVERS & KENT

BROOKE STREET, HOLBORN

1793–9 RAMSDEN, W & H (no 7)

1811–34 RAMSDEN, H & R (no 7)
1839–51 RAMSDEN Richard & Son (no 7)
1865–8 RAMSDEN, LANKESTER & EVANS (no 7)

CASTLE STREET

1784 BRACEBRIDGE & Son
1790s BOYLSTON Thomas & Co
1791–2 BRACEBRIDGE & Co
1794 BRACEBRIDGE A & W
1798–1815 BANKS John
1817 BANKE Geo & Co
1823–4 BANKES Geo & Co
1829 BANKES, G & C
1830 BANKES, G

COLE HARBOUR / COLDHARBOUR

1713–29 CHINNALL, T
1732–4 SCHRODER & BURMESTER
1732–41 WILFORD, J
1742–8 WILFORD & EADE
1743 CHIMMER, T
1747–9 SCHUTTE, C
1754–9 EADES John
1758–75 EDE John (no 1)
1759–63 SCHUTTE & RAVENCAMP
1765–6 KETTLER John
1768–74 KETTLER Cornelius (no 2)
1775–84 MOXHAM James (no 2)
1784–99 HENLOCK & DEWES (no 1)

COLLEGE HILL

1729–35 KIDD, R
1732 FRENCH, WOWEN & FENWICK
1736 HANKIN, J
1738 KIDD

1754 COPE & COE
1754 CORBETT, T & P
1754–9 WOWEN & FENWICK
1759 COAPE John
1761–3 FENWICK, M
1761–2 COOPE & JARMAN
1765 SMITH Francis
1772 FENWICK & BISHOP
1778–99 GROB John-Ernst (no 11)
1789–92 KING & SCHRODER (no 9)
1792–9 SCHRODER Herman (no 9)
1811 GROB, J
1811–21 SCHRODER Herman & Son (no 9)

DISTAFF LANE

1714 ASHURST, R
1728 ASHURST, T & W
1747–9 HORNBY, PAYNE & GILHART
1749 ILLINS, H
1754 ASHURST, T
1754 HOMAN, J
1754 ORTON John
1756 GRAMLICH, A
1756–62 HALLIDAY, R
1759–79 HORTON John (no 6)
1763–9 COAPE & JARMAN
1774–83 JARMAN Nathaniel (no 8)
1771–1815 BRUCKER George & Son (no 1)
1779–80 HORTON, MARMADUKE & KERTON (no 6)
1783–99 BELL James & Co (no 6)
1789–98 SIKES John & Co (no 8)
1794 SLACK, WALKER & SIKES
1811–5 HENLOCK, DEWS & Co (no 8)
1811 BANKES, FRIEND & Co

1817–24 BANKES Charles & Co
(C & G) (no 6)

EARL STREET

1785 BALLINGER Robert
1811 STOEVER John
1811 STROVER & BELL (no 15)

FRIDAY STREET

1750–2 HOMAN John
1757–68 WALKER John (no 47)
1769–80 WALKER John (no 16)
1772 PAYNE, S
1782 PIERCY, James jun
1789–90s WALKER Robert (no 16)

Gt TOWER STREET

1790s CAMMEYIER Charles (no 16)

Gt TRINITY LANE

1727–30 UNDERWOOD, J
1746–7 CHILDE & BUCKLEY
1750 BUCKLEY, S
1750 CHILDE, C
1754 CHILD & BUCKLEY
1762 FLAGMAN, H
1784–98 CAMMEYER Charles
(no 16)

HOLBORN HILL

1846 TRINGHAM Joseph & Son

JOINER'S HALL BUILDINGS

1724 ATKINS, A
1737 WRIGHT, L
1752 BLUNT, Sir H & JOHNSON
1761–2 BLUNT, Sir C, W & H
1763–9 BLUNT, Sir Charles
1779–80 BISHOP George & Samuel
(no 3)
1782 BISHOP, G & S, &
BLUNSTONE
1784 GRIFFIN George
1789–2 TRAVERS Benjamin & Co
(no 2)
1790 BELL & KRUGER
1791–2 BELL John
1792–5 HOMEWOOD Thomas
1792 BELL & Co
1796–9 BELL James
1797–9 HARRIS & ROBINSON
1809–17 FENN Thomas (no 2)

KNIGHT RIDER STREET

1741 INCE, P
1752 HALE, P
1759 LINDE Andrew
1764 BUTLER, J
1772–5 TURNER Barnard (no 5)

LABOUR-IN-VAIN HILL

1735 BOWLES & SCHRODER
1740 COOK, T
1748 BARNSTON & HORTON
1756–60 RIDER, J
1760 HALE, RIDER, GARLE &
RIDER
1766–9 RIDER & GARLE (no 3)
1769–72 RIDER Jacob (no 1)
1775–92 WALKER Robert (no 1)
1780 HAHN & SELDENSHO (no 3)
1784 HAHN & QUADENO
1789–92 HAHN & LEE (no 3)
1791 HALES & LEE
1792 LEE Joseph
1794 HAHN & Son

LAMBETH HILL

1740 BRACEBRIDGE, A
1752–5 GOEBELL, J & G
1759–66 GOEBELL John Gerrard
1762 GOEBELL, G & A
1777–94 BRACEBRIDGE, A & W

LIME STREET

1729 LEWIS, P & T
1732–4 LEWIS & NELSON
1759–74 LEWIS Thomas (no 42)
1761–9 MARTIN & LEWES (no 42)
1774–7 MARTIN & Co (no 42)
1776–80 SHUM & Son (no 42)
1784–92 SHUM & GLOVER (no 42)
1794–7 SHUM & GIBSON (no 42)
1802 GIBSON, T
1813–7 GIBSON & Co (no 42)

LITTLE CARTER LANE

1754 NICHOLS & TOMLINSON
1771 GARLE & HILTON
1776, 94 GARLE Tho & John (no 24)
1794–6 SEIFFE & SMITH (no 24)
1798–9 KENDALL, R H (no 24)
1813–7 CHURCH & STOVER (no 25)

LOWER THAMES STREET

1735–8 HARTOP & ROTSHOUCH
(Tower Hill)
1795 TOWGOOD & DANVERS
(Harp Lane)
1832 GEORGE & HARWOOD

MINCING LANE

1544 BOSSIGNE Cornelius ?
1544 CHESTER William, Sir ?
1544 GARDENOR John ?
1544 MUNSEY ?
1544 POYNS Fernando ?
1585–92 MYDDLETON Thomas, Sir
1732 ASHURST, W & T
1839 HASLEHURST William (no 13)

1839 HEWITT William (no 4)

OLD CHANGE

1789–2 KNOWLYS Thomas (no 28)
1796 KELLER Philip
1811 BAUMAN, G S (no 28)
1815 DIXON & HECKMAN (no 28)
1817 GOULET, A & Co

OLD FISH STREET

1729–30 NEW, E
1748 COOPER, H
1755–67 BELLMAN, H
1762 CONSTANTINE, H
1765–72 CONSTANTIEN Hardwick
(no 6)
1770–92 PIERCE(Y) James (no 6)
1792 PEARKES James (no 6)
1794–9 BALLENGER Robert & Co
(no 6)
1796–9 HAHN & Son (no 3)
1815 CHURCH & STOVER
1816 CHURCH Elizabeth
1829 BANKS

OLD FISH STREET HILL

1794 BALLENGER Rob (no 6)
1796–8 WALKER Robert (no 1)
1797–1807 MARTINEAU David &
Peter, & Mr SPURRELL
1815–7 HAHN, G H (no 3)

PAULS WHARF

1724 BUTLER Henry
1727 FIRMSTONE Samuel
1735 BERKLEY, J & J
1742 BERKLEY & INCE
1742 FULLER Thomas
1743–6 CHAPMAN, W
1754–9 WRIGHT & PLUMB
1754–5 BARRATT, C
1755 POWER, J
1759 RICHTER Jacob
1759 BARRATT & JEMMITT
1759–66 BERKLEY &
BRACEBRIDGE
1761–6 JEMMITT, T
1763–88 HALLIDAY Robert
1767 VAUGHAN, J
1768–9 BRACEBRIDGE & GIBBS
1777 VAUGHAN & HORTON
1779–84 TURNER Barnard (no 8)
1781 TURNER & SWINEY
1786 VAUGHAN, J & B
1789–92 BOYLSTON Thomas
<1795 LEAR Henry

PUDDLE DOCK

1728 JEMMET & REHME
1729 JEMMETT, E & E

1730 MOSTYN & PAYNE
1753 HALLIDAY & PEIRCY
1755 WEIMAN, G
1760–2 TIEHMAN & SAMLER
1766 PAYNE & BISHOP
1771–2 PAYNE, J & S
1771–9 COOKE Thomas
1772 SAMLER, H
1777 PRESTON, T
1777 TURNER & LINDENBURG
1781 BRACEBRIDGE, J, jun

QUEEN STREET

1754 DANDRIDGE, J & C
1754–63 NASH William
1759–66 DANDRIDGE, J
1766 INNECKEN, ASHERMAN &
  HOPKINS
1766–8 BARTELS Henry (no 35)
1767–8 DEKEWER John (no 49)
1768–9 DANDRIDGE & BLUNT
  (no 36)
1769–70 DEKEWER & PERKINS
  (no 49)
1771 POOLE, S
1774–9 BLUNT Walter (no 36)
1776–80 SEDGEWICK & SPRADO
  (no 35)
1777 FIXSEN, F
1777 KNOR, Frederick
1781 TILLET, W
1784–5 TRAVERS Benjamin (no 36)
1784–92 DAVIS Robert (no 35)
1789–92 KING & BANKS (no 49)
1790s KNOWLES Thomas & Co
  (no 35)
1792–1807 TRAVERS Benjamin
  (no 36)
1794–9 WORSLEY & HEINEKIN
  (no 37)
1794–7 PAKEMAN James (no 57)
1794 SEVERN, B
1796–9 HAWKSWORTH &
  PRESCOTT (no 49)
1797 SEVERN, SMITH & COX
1797–9 ACKROYD, T (no 35)
1813–7 DINGWALL James (Maiden
  Lane)
1815–7 EDELMAN & Son (no 35)
1820 CONWAY & Co
1823 YOUNG Florence & Co
  (no 61½)

SHOEMAKERS ROW

1767–8 DEARBERG Seagmund
  (no 3)
1769–72 WAKEFORD John (no 3)

ST ANDREWS HILL

1772–94 SAMLER & Son

1776–8 TURNER Barnard (no 8)
1778 COOK Thomas (no 21)
1778–83 PRESTON Thomas (no 5)
1791 SAMLER, H & W
1793–1817 SAMLER, W & R
1823–4 SAMLER Wm

ST BENNETS HILL

1732 BUTLER & Co
1768–9 HALE & RIDER (no 17)
1774–5, 90–6 GARLE Tho & John
  (no 17)
1796 BRACEBRIDGE Walter
1797–1817 SMITH & SEIFFE (no 17)
1815–6 SMITH, J

ST DUNSTAN'S HILL

1612–4 HOSKOM Arthur
1725 SODEN, T
1799 DARKNELL & HOWE (no 4)

ST MARTIN'S LANE

1754–9 NELSON James
1760 SCHUTTE, RAVENCAMP &
  INKEN
1766 RAVENCAMP & KETTLER
1767–79 RAVENCAMP Frederick
  (no 18)
1784–99 GLOVER David (no 19)
1794 GLOVER, D & T
1811 MILLIKEN & ACKROYD
  (no 19)
1815 ACKROYD Thomas (no 19)

ST MARY HILL

1783 FRAISER
1815 HOLNESS Joseph (7 Cross
  Lane)

UPPER THAMES STREET

1722 UNDERWOOD, J (Trigg Stairs)
1722–3 REEME, CROOK &
  JAMMETT
1725 TARNNAIES, J (Three Cranes)
1725–33 BLUNT & WRIGHT
1727–9 KIDD, BELITHA & HARBIN
  (Brick Hill Lane)
1728–9 FELLOWS, T (Five Foot
  Lane)
1731 BURMESTER, L (Lawrence
  Poultney Lane)
<1738 KIDD
1738–40 TORRIANA, J (Three
  Cranes)
1739 BLOOM, GABHERT &
  STEPHAN (Addle Hill)
1740 ROTSHOUCH & TORRIANA
1741 ROTSHOUCH & TORRIANA
  (Steel Yard)

1741–2 BERKLEY, J (Baynards
  Castle)
<1746 EMERSON, Thomas
1746–7 TRULOCH & NASH (Three
  Cranes)
1747–9 BLOOM, F (Addle Hill)
1748–52 LEACHMAN, J
  (Fishmongers Hall)
1750–3 NASH, W (Three Cranes)
1753 NICHOL & HORTON (Five
  Foot Lane)
1752–3 MARSH & HARDACRE
  (Queenhythe)
1754 BARTELS & MASON (High
  Timber Street)
1754–9 LEACHMAN John (nr the
  bridge)
1755 WRIGHT, P (Somers Key)
1756–7 MARSH, J (Five Foot Lane)
1759–70 QUELCH Richard (no 207)
1760 BLUNT, H (Lawrence Poultney
  Lane)
1760–3 RAWLINSON, DAWSON,
  NEWMAN & HASE
  (Fishmongers Hall)
1762 SMITH & LEHMAN (Brick Hill
  Lane)
1763 RAWLINSON, T & others
  (Steel Yard)
1763–6 PLUMBE Charles
1766 JONES Richard
1766 HALE & PYCROFT (Vintners
  Hall)
<1767 PAYNE
1767 BARTLETT
1767–9 BILL & BURTON (Brick Hill
  Lane)
1768 ELLIS Barnaby (no 34)
1768 HASE, H (Fishmongers Hall)
1768–9 JEMMITT & VAUGHAN
  (no 25)
1768–9 HALE & PYCROFT (no 68)
1768–72 PAYNE John
1771 GARLE (Kiln Lane)
1771 HELMKEN & RATCLIFF
  (Broken Wharf)
1772 NICHOL, J (Five Foot Lane)
1772 PYCROFT, W (Vintners Hall)
1773 PYCROFT William (no 68)
1773–6 HASE Henry (no 127)
1776 WHITEMAN, J
1776 MARSH John, broker (no 203)
1777 GIBB, C
1779–80 TILLETT William (no 68)
1779–80 VAUGHAN John (no 25)
1780 LABORDE Samuel (no 207)
1780 CARR & LEAR
1781 GIBBS
1781 INNECKEN, C
1781 LABORDE, S

1783–9 VAUGHAN John (no 25)
1784 ANSELL & PLATER (no 34)
1784 BARBER John & Joseph (no 78)
1784 BRACEBRIDGE &
   STREATFIELD (Rutland Pl)
1789 BARBER John (no 78)
1789 BRACEBRIDGE & Co
   (Rutland Pl)
1789 FOX Edward (no 68)
1789 HESE Ann (no 127)
1789 HOMEWOOD Thomas (no 34)
1789–94 FAWKES Edward (no 68)
1789–99 SYKES Luke (no 180)
1790–2 SHAW Benjamin, cooper
   (no 203)
1790–3 HASE Anne (no 127)
1790–7 BANKES John & Co (no 202)
1791–4 WIPLE & BEESWANK
   (no 240)
1792– BARBER John & Joseph
   (no 73)
1792– TRAVERS Benjamin & Co
   (no 2)
1793 SYKES, L (Brick Hill Lane)
1794–5 FRIEAKE & Co (no 207)
1794 KNOWLYS Thomas (no 78)
1794–9 WALTON & DETMAR
   (no 127)
1795 KNOWLES, T (Brick Hill Lane)
1795 KING & BANKS
c1795 WATSON Jacob Kruger
1796 KNIES & PRITZLER (no 78)
1796–9 NICHOLL John (no 68)
1797 KNOWLES Thomas (no 78)
1797–9 WIPLE & Son (no 240)
1797–9 SHAW & CHURCH, coopers
   (no 203)
1800 FRIECKE & ENDELMAN
1801 GROBB
1807–32 SMITH John (no 50)
1810–17 REYNOLDS John (no 68)
1811 RITHERDON Samuel (no 202)
1811 FENN Thomas (no 78)
1811 SMITH & BROWN (no 50)
1811–7 FRIEAKE, H&S (no 205)
1813 PENN, T
1813 RITHERDON & SUTHNIER
   (no 202)
1813–5 TROLLOPE, H & Co
1815 COSLETT & SOUTHMIER
1815 EAMER, T H (no 240)
1815 DANVERS, C (Rutland Pl)
1815–21 BASSANO & Co (no 180)
1815–7 ELLIOTT & RUCKER (no 44)
1817 RITHERDON & Co (no 202)
1823–4 RUCKER, M.D (no 44)
1827 EAMER, T H (no 243)
1834 SMITH & Son (no 50)
1834 BANKES Geo (no 16)
1835–36 SMITH Charles (no 50)

1838–40 SMITH Charles (no 203)
1840–51 SMITH & TYERS (no 203)

WATER LANE
1739 ROWBOTHOM & LILKENDEY
1748–56 RAVENCAMP, F
1749–51 HORMAN & SAMLER
1754–6 SAMLER, H
1756 GEBBART & HAMMOND
1757 DAWSON & CLADEN
1758–71 SAMLER Harman (no 26)
1762 SCHUTTE & RAVENCAMP
1766–72 LEAR Henry (no 25)

WHITEFRIARS
1718 EVANS John
…Fleet Street…
1745 PALMER & WYATT
…Lombard Street…
1746 ECKSON, N
1758 HARDACRE, M
1761–6 INNECKEN, ASHEMAN &
   HOPKINS
1766–71 CAMMEYER, C
1786–98? CARR William
1791–2 KUHN George & Martin
1792 ROBERTS & DAVIES
…Essex Street…
1755 RIDER, J
1759 CREMER, SWITZER &
   MOSTAR
…Silver Street…
1783 CARR Frederick

WORCESTER PLACE
1724–33 CLAYTON, T
1769–72 GREENHOW James (no 2)

EAST END

ALIE STREET
1773 RICHARDS Andrew
1777–83 WALKER John (no 8)
1789 MUDDLE Edward (no 8)
1789–99 MUM Henry (no 12)
1790s LAWRENCE & Co
1790–2 BLAMIRE Edward (no 8)
1791–9 TRAPP Gregory
1796–8 BLAMIRE Edward (no 30)
1799 BLAMIRE Edward (no 50)
1811 CAMMEYER Chas. (no 9)
1820–1 LIST, J
1823–52 BOWMAN Frederick & Son
   (no 27)
1829–33 WICHART, D
1846 HAGEN, E & Co (no 11)
1851 GREENWOOD Thomas (no 11)
1865–8 HICKS, Thomas & Francis
   (no 11)

ANGEL ALLEY
1719 LANE, S
1727 WARREN & MARTIN
1729 WARREN, MARTIN & LANE
1733–49 BROMWELL John
1735 SCHUTTE, C
1746–9 LANE, J
1748–59 COOPE Richard
1750 BROWN, M
1754 TURQUAND John
1755–63 BECKMAN Nicholas
1758–84 COOPE John
1759–65 SUHRING John Christian
1754–60 TITIEN & SHEERING
1763 BRIENEGER, M
1763–92 SUHRING John Christian &
   John Henry
1766–72 RIDER Frederick
1773 BRUNIGES
1777 PYCROFT, W
1778–83 PYCROFT & PAYNE
1779–83 COOPE, CHARLESON &
   Co
1786 PYCROFT & RAIKES
1789–92 COOPE, CHARLESON,
   COOPE & COOPE
1789–1815 SAMLER & FERRERS
1789–90s PYCROFT & WILSON
1794 COOPE, J & Sons
1794–6 PYCROFT & WARDE
1798 PYCROFT, WARDE &
   PYCROFT
1798 SAMBLER & Co
1813 PAXTON, G
1823–4 WALTON & FAIRBANK
1829–30 WALTON, J

ANTHONY STREET
1821–77 GUNDLACH Johann
   (no 102)

BACK CHURCH LANE
1823–4 SCUDDER Gerrard (no 8)

BACK LANE
1834 BROWNE H N
1834 KYMER John
1834–41 LANGE Nicholas
1851?–61 DRAKE George
Bath Terrace…
1805–24 HOLTHOUSE & DETMAR
1826–33 HOLTHOUSE Carsten
1865–8 FAIRRIE BROS & Co

BELL LANE
1736–41 STEPHENS & KNUST
   (Coxes Square)
1748–9 GOEBELL, J & G (Coxes
   Square)
1755 SCHERER, B (Coxes Square)

1814 CONWAY, PHILLIPS & RAW
1816 MARTENS, I

BETTS STREET

1758 WACKERBARTH & LARKIN
1763 WACKERBARTH & GAY
1766 WACKERBARTH Diederick
1771 CLARKE, H
1772 CLINKER & PELL
1776 WACKERBARTH & BATGER
1777–89 DETMAR Joseph
1779–84 WACKERBARTH, BATGER
    & DETTMERE
1781–94 CLINKER Aaron
1779–89 WACKERBARTH, Son &
    DETMER
1790s WACKERBARTH, MAUD &
    Co
1794 ENGELL & WILSON
1794–9 WACKERBARTH George
1811 WACKERBARTH, DETMAR &
    CHURCH
1814 ORANGE, HARRISON &
    SCHULTZ
1817 CROSLAND Wm & Co
1817 WALE Wm & Co
1823–4 BROWN Henry (no 10)
1823–39 COOP(E) John
1823–34 GAVILLER & WALES
1831 GAVILLER & Co
1834 BRIANT & Co
1841 WILLIAMS Jos (no 42)
1846 COOPE, O E

BLACK BULL ALLEY

1861 "Sugar Bakery in Black Bull
    Alley"

BREEZERS HILL

1758–63 LUDEKIN, C
1762 DIRS, C
1763 PECKERSON &
    HOLTZMEYER
1776 PAULHAM & BLACK
1778 DIRS Carsten
1793 L(A/O)MAN, C
1797–9 LORMEN Christian
1799 DIRS Court
1815–17 DIRS Carsten
1817 BOCKEN Henry Christian
1821–4 HOLTHOUSE & DETMAR
1834–68 HALL & BOYD

BRICK LANE

1757–8 CHARLESON, L
1776 SCHUCHAT, H
1777 CHARLESON, L
1777 PRITZLER, T
1789–1815 WALKER John (no 211)
1794 WALKER & AUNSLEY

1815–34 WALKER William (no 211)
1821 HENKINS, C & Co

BROADWAY (Goulston Street)

1861 MARTINEAU Peter & Son

BUCKLE STREET

1723 HOPPENER & HASLEAR
1726 BUDGEN, T
1733 BRIDGE & EDE
1748 HALE & CROSBY
1755–71 CROSBY George
1773–83 CROSBY & STERLING
1784 CROSBY George
1789–98 MUM Henry & Co
1790–9 CRAVEN John & Co

CABLE STREET

1766 BELL, W
1794 EGGARS & Co
1815 FERRERS & WETHERELL
    (Princes Pl)
1823–4 HINCKEN & Co
1834 LANGE, N
1841 HINKENS Claus

CHARLES STREET

1823–4 BRIEBACH Albert

CHARLOTTE STREET

1798 HOLZMEYER
1829 FRIEND & BODEN

CHRISTIAN STREET

1807–68 MARTINEAU David (no 6)
1813 ROBINSON & SCHROEDER
1820–30 SCHROEDER, G & Co
1830 CLARK, H
1834 SCHROEDER & HINCKEN
1834–51 KUCK Peter (no 5)
1834–41 WOLGEMUTH Conrad
    (no 9)
1834–5 BOULNOIS & Co
1835 BONUS & Co
1841 SCHRODER & Co
1844–56 SCHWINGE Deiderick
    (no 1)
1846–51 SCHRODER, HINCKEN &
    Co (no 7)
1846–68 WAINWRIGHT &
    GADESDEN (no 4)
1865–73 KUCK Peter (no 3)
1865–81 WOLGEMUTH Conrad
    (no 11)
1881 MARTINEAU, D & Son

CHURCH LANE

1761–8 MacKECLEN Richard
1769–72 GREENHOW James
1775 DAVEY & HOUNSOM

1776–7 TURQUAND John
1777 GOEBELL, J
1777–84 DOORMAN John W
1783 GOEBELL Gerrard
1784 HUDSON Thomas
1789–1815 DOORMAN &
    HODGSON
1790–9 WALTON & WICKE
1793 COSLETT William
1794 SEVERN, B
1794–1824 WICKE George
1798 HODGSON Thomas
1813–31 HODGSON Thomas & Son
    (no 8)
1815–29 SEVERN, KING & Co
1817 HOLTZMEYER, H
1829 SEVERN & Co
1829 SKUDDER Gerard Wilkins
1830–65 FAIRRIE Bros & Co
1830–51 BOWMAN Charles
1834 FAIRRIE, ANDERSON & Co
1868 WOHLGEMUTH Conrad
    (no 59)

CHURCH STREET, MENT

1809–15 ALMEROTH, H & Co
1817–24 BURNELL, GEISS & Co
    (no 12)
1830 GEORGE, S & R (Deal Street)
1830–4 BURNELL Richard & Son
1868 DAKIN & BRYANT (no 12)

CLEVELAND STREET

1846 WOOD Martin (no 5)

DENMARK STREET

1811 KEATES Robert
1811–17 WADDINGTON, CROOK &
    THOMPSON
1815 CROSLAND Wm & Co
1815 DUCROZ & SHEY
1817 GAVELLIR & WELLS (no 4)
1817–24 GEORGE Christian
1817 SHEE John
1817 SUTHMEYER H (no 6)
1818–46 SCHLENCKER Thomas
1820 TRAPPS
1823–35 SCHWARTZ Jacob
1823–4 WADDINGTON & Co (no 2)
1826 BEIHL, T
1826–41 THOMPSON & KUCK
1830–4 KUCK, J
1834 MUENCH, John
1834–6 THOMPSON & Co
1838–68 BRIEBACH & MOGGE
    (no 11)
1844–51 BRADEN Herman (no 12)
1846 SCHLENKER, J
1865–8 PARKER Fredrick (no 12)

DOCK STREET (SALT PETRE BANK)

(Now Salt Petre Bank)
1722 FISHER, G
1729 CORDIS, F
1730 CORDIS, MAJOR & OXLEY
1731 CORDIS, DAVIES, DAVIS & HARDING
1743 BOSWELL, T
1746 BROWN & AYRES
1752 HESSE, G
1793 FISHER, E
(Now Dock Street)
1811 AUSTIN Daniel
1811–17 MEYER & HINCKEN
1813–29 HINCKEN, M & Co
1815 AUSTIN & GLENNIE
1816–21 SCHLENCKER, G & Son
1820–6 DEMPSEY & RICE (REIS) (no 14)
1821 HENKINS, C
1823–4 CROUCHER & BISHOP
1823–4 JONES Hart (no 12)
1823–4 SCHLENCKER George & John (no 13)
1823–4 SCHLENCKER George & Son (no 9&10)
1827–30 JONAS & AARON
1829–35 SCHLENCKER Jacob
1830 BISHOP, M
1830–4 JONAS, H & Co
1830 STEWERT & Co
1830–4 SCHLENCKER, J & G
1831 SMITH
1831–4 STEWART & SCHIBBEN
1834 LIENAU, F & Co
1834–41 HODGSON & Son
1844–51 HODGSON John (no 5)
1861–8 HARRISON John (no 5)

DUNCAN STREET

1799 CRAVEN & MUM
1806 CRAVEN James & BOWMAN Fred
1806 CRAVEN Matthew
1811–17 BRADBURNE & FRYER (no 12)
1812–7 CRAVEN & BOWMAN
1821–5 CRAVEN, J & M
1823–4 FRYER & ROHRS (no 12)
1829–34 FRYER & Co
1830–5 BOWMAN, F
1838 BOWMAN Francis & Son
1838 CRAVEN, H
1839–40 BOWMAN Frederick
1839–46 CRAVEN & LUCAS

DUNK STREET

1826 WARDS/WOODS, G
1838–9 ZABELL Frederick William

1855–82 SCHWIER Ernest Louis Victor (no 39)
1883–96 SCHWIER Charles, Ernest, Walter (no 39)
1897–1961 MARTINEAU (no 39) (and King(Ed)ward Street)

EAST SMITHFIELD

1726 IRESON & MACKLEAN (Upper)
1738 BACKMAN & CAMDEN (Nightingale Lane)
1769 COOK George (no 4 lower)
1772 BRODT (Parrot Alley)
1777 KRIETEMEYER, J (Nightingale Lane)
1784 DROST John Alto
1791 KRIETEMEYER, A & F (Nightingale Lane)
1796–9 FISHER Edward (no 90 upper)

FASHION STREET

1784 PYCROFT & PAYNE
1792– BECKMAN Nicholas F (no 18)

FIELDGATE STREET

1736 BRISSAULT
1742–52 BRISSAULT & TURQUAND
1758–74 TURQUAND Leonard
1760–3 BRISSAULT, J jun
1771–4 TURQUAND James Lewis
1811 BELL James
1817 FRIEND James & Edward
1821–31 BODEN, W
1821–51 FRIEND & BODEN (no 17)
1846 FRIEND, J B
1865–8 HODGE Sydney B (no 17)

FINCH STREET

1814–5 BRIENLECK, G
1818 WESTFAHLEN & SIEME
1821–4 BUTCHER & JORDAN
1823–4 JORDAN Thomas (no 8)
1827 STOKES & STEVENS
1827–46 BURNBOOM William (no 12)
1839–41 BRADEN Herman (no 14)
1839–41 HOLMAER Claus (no 13)
1846 BOWDEN & Co
1846 DOSSCHER Geoffrey (no 14)
1846 BURMBOOM, N
1848–51 BURNBOOM, Mrs H (no 12)
1851–3 BRADEN Charles (no 14)
1851–60 HOLMAEAR Henry (no 13)
1851 PICKEL Conrad (no 8)

FLOWER & DEAN STREET

1802 STEPHENS & LONSDALE

GLASSHOUSE STREET (WHITES YARD)

1851 Glasshouse Street Sugar House

GLOUCESTER STREET

1811–15 TEMPERLEY, N (no 34)
1823–4 TEMPERLEY Nicholas (no 35)
1830 MUHM, M
1851 PRIGGEN Jacob (no 35)
1868 MARTIN Thomas (no 33)

GOODMAN'S STILE

1794 TRAPP, GREGORY & Co
1811 TRAPP & HODGSON
1815 HODSON Thomas & Son
1834–6 HODGSON Thomas, jun
1851–68 ELERS & MORGAN

GOODMANS YARD

1777 HAWES John & Co
1830 BURKETT & MILBOURN

GOULSTON STREET

1813 MARTINEAU, P
1815–68 MARTINEAU Peter & Son (no 5)
1824 WASMUTH George Christian

GOWERS WALK

1794 WALTON & WICKE
1798 WALTON & WITTE
1815 ROBERTS, WANGEMANN & Co (no 12)
1833 BOWMAN
1834 BACKHAM & Co
1841 RACKHAM & PRIEST
1846–52 PUEST & WICKE
1865–8 MUHM & MULLER (no 2)

GRAVEL LANE, HOUNDSDITCH

1754 IRESON, D
1759 IRESON & WARD
1763–9 IRESON, WARD & LANG
1789–98 SLACK & WALKER
1809–11 SLACK & BURGESS
1815–17 SLACK, BURGESS & BECKWITH (no 108)
1834 WIDDER & Co

GT GARDEN STREET

1747 PHILLIPSON, C
1757–69 TURQUAND Paul
1771–2 TURQUAND, P & L
1772 CHESMER, T
1783–99 EGGARS Henry (no 3)
1789–99 LEAR, G & Co (no 13)

1811–15 LEAR & COBDEN (no 13)
1811 WALKER William (no 8)
1815–24 MANN Alex (no 6)
1815–17 SEARANCKE Wm
1816 BROOKS, HARRISON & Co
1823–4 HARRISON & BIEHL
1865 CRAVEN John (no 3)

GT PRESCOTT STREET

1798–9 VULLIAMY Lewis
1798–9 HARBUSCH Harman
1798–9 BOTT John
1798–9 LAWRENCE & Co
1798–9 DAMES Richard
1823 LILCKENDEY George
1846 HENRICKSON, H (no 3)

HALIFAX STREET

1807 DIRS John Court
1838 ZABELL

HENEAGE STREET

1839–65 BACKER Henry (no 1)

HOOPER SQUARE

1795 RHODE, E & M
1815 HINRICKSON, R
1830 DREYER John
1844–6 GOODHART, E
1846–51 GOODHART & PATRICK
1865 GOODHART Charles Emanuel

JOHN STREET

1844–6 HOLTZMEYER, H R

KING EDWARD STREET

1823–6 HOREY John (no 36)
1897–1961 MARTINEAU (no 13)
    (and Dunk Street)

LAMBETH STREET

1734 SCHUTTE, C
1738 SMETH & Co
1740 BARKER & CARTER
1757 WALKER & MATTHEWS
1763 BUCKLEY SCHULERMAN
1789–98 HALL & FISHER
1792–8 WALTERS & FISHER
1793–6 DEWES & ANSELL (no 77)
1795 FISHER Walter
1795 RICHDALE James
1797–8 LUCAS & MARTIN
1798–9 MERTENS Lear
1799 FISHER John
1799 TRAPP John
1806–1815 DAVIS & SUTTON
    (no 81)
1806 STEWARD & HALL
1806 TRAPP Widow & HODGSON
    John

1811 WALTON & FAIRBANK
1811–15 DAMES, PAXTON &
    DAMES (no 80)
1813–5 DAVIS, W
1815 WALTON John (Johnson's Ct)
1817 DAMES, RASTUS & Co
1817–24 WALTON, FAIRBANK &
    WALTON (no 77)
1830 PAXTON & Co
1834 WALTON, John
1851–68 ELERS & MORGAN (no 47)

LEMAN STREET

1724 WYNE, E
1729 WASTFIELDE & BROMLEY
1746–61 SCHUMACKER, F
1748–61 TIELHEN Christian
1749 PHILLIPSON & HILL
1754–9 PHILLIPSON Christopher
1760 MACKELEAN, R
1760 SMITH
1763 HESS, J
1763 SMITH & PHILLIPSON
1766–9 SMITH & MATTHEW
1767 SPARMAN, F
1771–7 SHUM, G
1771–9 CONSTANTIEN Hardwick
    (no 66)
1772–9 MATTHEW Job (no 4)
1783–92 PARRY Nicholas (no 4)
1784 CONSTANTIEN &
    LAWRENCE (no 66)
1784–98 VULLIAMY & BOTT
    (no 65)
1789–97 MILLER John (no 59)
1790s BOTT John (no 64)
1791–8 ROHDE Major (no 86)
1793 SHUM & GIBSON
1793–7 NASH Thomas (no 4)
1794 LAWRENCE, VULLIAMY &
    BOTT (nos 65 & 66)
1798 LAWRENCE & Co
1798–9 ROHDE Major
1798–9 CRAVEN Matthew (no 4)
1798–1806 HARBUSCH Harman &
    Co
1799 WILLIAM & Co
1802–6 LAWRENCE Richard &
    WALTON Henry
1805 ROHDE Major
1806 HENDRICKSON Nicholas
1806 ROHDE, M J & ROHDE
1811 HESSE Gabriel
1811 HARBUSCH Harman (no 59)
1811 WADDINGTON Samuel
    (no 13)
1811–17 MARTINEAU & REID
    (no 4)
1813–6 MARTINEAU & Co

1813–24 LAWRENCE & CARLILL
    (no 65)
1814 REID, T
1815 DANES, R
1815 HARBUSCH & Co (no 60)
1815 LAWRENCE & Co (no 65)
1815–7 ROHDE Major & Co (no 84)
1819 ROHDE, M & Son
1821 ROHDE, M
1822–7 ROHDE Major & Co (no 64)
1823–4 WICHART & Co (no 59)
1829–34 COTTON & THELLUSEN
    (no 84)
1831–5 COTTON & Co
1834 DAMES, CR (no 18)
1834–9 WOOLSEY George M (no 4)
1834–46 DAVIS John (no 64)
1839 COTTON Benjamin (no 87)
1839 LAWRENCE Richard Henshaw
    & MORTON William (no 68)
1841 COTTON & Co (no 87)
1841–6 GADSDEN, J & Son (no 4)
1851–68 CRAVEN & LUCAS (no 12)
1851–68 WAINWRIGHT &
    GADESDEN (nos 56 & 57)
1851–68 DAVIS John (nos 113 & 114)
1852–67 BOWMAN'S (no 78)
1865–8 GOODHART Charles
    Emanuel (nos 97 & 98)
1868 DAKIN & BRYANT (no 46)

MANSELL STREET

1739–41 DUKES, N (Somerset Street)
1749 EGGARS, J (Somerset Street)
1753 JASPER, J (Somerset Street)
1766 SPALDING, SLACK &
    DOWNING
1768–9 SLACK, DOWNING & Co
1770 SLACK, T
1771 SPALDING, SLACK & HAWES
1778 SPALDING, SLACK, HAWES
    & WALKER
1780–99 HAWES, J (no 1)
1781–2 SLACK & HAWES
1790s DEWS & ANSELL
1792–1811 HAWES John & Co (no 1)
1830 BIRKET & Co
1834 BURKETT & SCHNIBBER
1839 WAGENER, J
1841 BROWN, H W (no 35)
1841–51 WAGENER John (no 3)
1846–51 COOPE Octavius Edward
    (no 2)
1848 SILBERBACH Charles F A

**MULBERRY STREET / UNION
STREET**

1819 SEVERN (KING) & Co

NELSON STREET

1814 CRAVEN, M
1821 CRAVEN, J & M
1821 CRAVEN & SHUTTE
1830 CRAVEN & LUCAS
1835 CRAVEN & Co

NEW ROAD

1789–92 DYON(S) Casten
1796–8 DETMAR John
1811 SEARANCKE William
1817 HOLTHOUSE & DETMAR
1817 MARTIN & Co
1817 NOETH & GOODHART
1820–4 LUCAS & MARTIN
1823–4 LANGE Nicolas
1823–4 SCHLENCKER Jacob (no 3)
1826 BARLOW & DOERING
1833 HOLTHOUSE Carsten

OLD FORD

1846 CHAPMAN Bros

OLD MONTAGUE ST

1811 WILKINS Gerard
1821–5 WIEBKIN, D
1825 PRATT, S
1846 FERRADAY & TANNER
 (no 17) (treacle)
1851 BOHLING Claus Henry (no 20)

OSBORN STREET

1732 BROMWELL, J (George Yard)
1777 COOPE, J
1789–92 CHARLESON Lawrence
 (Osborn Place)
1792–7 COOPE & Co
1793–4 PYCROFT & WARDLE
1798–9 COOPE John & Sons
1798–1821 DEWES & ANSELL
1799–1815 MARTIN & LUCAS
1806 DEWS, ANSELL, DEWS
1811–15 COOPE, J & J
1811–15 DEWS & ANSELL
1812 MARTIN Henry
1815–23 DETTMAR & Son
1816 COOPE, J
1817 COOPE John
1817 COOPE Joseph
1820 LUCAS & TOWNSEND
1820–1 COOPE, J & Co
1821 LUCAS & Co
1823–4 DEWES Robert & Christian
 (no 2)
1830–4 BULMER & ROHRS (no 8)
1830–1 DEWES & Co
1831 BULMER & Co
1831–4 FARMER James
1834 COOPE John
1834–41 BANKES George (no 2)

1844–6 DAMES & BOWMAN
1851–65 DAMES & Son (no 2)
1868 DAMES & Son (no 6)

PARSONS STREET

1748 RIMERS, BOSLEY & RODDY
1766–71 RITTENGER & FOSSEY
1771 WACKERBARTH, J
1777–80 DROST, J
1788 LILKENDEY, G
1793–1811 WACKERBARTH, G
 (no 44)
1797–1815 HARRISON &
 LILKENDEY (no 77)
1815–30 WACKERBARTH & Co
1816 SCHLENCKER, J
1821 HACKERBACK, M & Co
1830 CHURCH & Co
1834 CHURCH & KERSTING
1834 COLLING, Josh (no 44)
1834–46 WACKERBATH &
 COLLING (no 45)
1835 LILKENDEY, A
1840 KERSTING, J

PELL STREET

1783–1820 DETMAR George
1865–8 BRUXNER Michael Fredrick
 (no 14)

PENNINGTON STREET

1763–1800 DIRS Court
1777 DINGWALL, J
1783–1820 DETMAR George
1793 DIRS Cort
1846 GOODHART J & Son

PLEASANT ROW, MENT

1811 THOMAS, G (no 10)
1865 SCHWARTZ John (no 14)

PRINCES PLACE

1772–6 WACKERBARTH, D
1794–5 PARKER & PERRAM
1810–5 MARTINEAU David
1811 MARTINEAU & SPURRELL
1811–15 WETHERELL & FERRERS
1811–24 SARGEANT &
 MIDDLETON
1813–31 BOULNOIS, W
1815 WARREN Edw & Rbt
1815–21 TYLER, J
1815 ROBINSON & SCHRODER
1815–24 ROBINSON & KUCK
1815–17 SCHRODER Joseph
1816 TAYLOR, J
1819–30 SARGEANT & Co
1823–4 BOULNOIS Wm
1823–4 MARTINEAU David & Sons
1823–4 SCHRODER Josh & Son

1825–7 SARGEANT, J & R
1829–30 HASLEM, B
1830 MARTINEAU, D
1831–5 MARTINEAU, D & Son
1839–46 MARTINEAU David Henry
1844–6 HINCKEN & Co
1851 KUCK Peter

PRINCES SQUARE

1772 BATGER, H
1790s MAUD Samuel (no 19)
1791 BARKER John
1791–7 PARKER & PERRIN
1818–20 TYLER & BATGER
1831 KING Frederick Benjamin

PRINCES STREET

1838 ZABELL

RED LION STREET

1834–46 CRAVEN & LUCAS (no 8)

ROSE LANE

1731 BRISSAULT, J

ROSEMARY LANE

1740–2 WHITE & RAPP (Marine
 Square)
1750 RIPP & WHITE (Marine
 Square)
1798–9 WACKERBATH Dederick
1815 VERDENHALM William
 (10 White's Yd)
1821 LAWRENCE & Co (Seven Star
 Court)
1829–30 BACKLER or BOCKLEY, M
 (Glass House Yard)

RUPERT STREET

1725–32 WYNN Ed
1728 ROTSHOUCH, P & N
1729 HARTOP & ROTSHOUCH
1730 LORANCE, W
1732–9 PARTIS, Capt
1732–53 HARTOP
1732–53 WOOD Matthew
1739 HENDERSON & CORDIS
1743 JURMER, J
1744–9 JENNER, J
1746 CHEEK Thomas
1749 LONG, J
1750 RIMERS, G
1751–73 DEARSON, B
1753 LONG
1753 MACKELEAN & BURMAN
1759–71 LONG John
1761 HALL, J
1766–70 HESS Joseph
1770 DROST Otto
1777 RICHLADE, J

1781 ROBINS, R
1789–92 NASH Thomas (no 34)
1790–9 DAMES Richard (cooper)
   (no 7)
1790–8 WILMOT & POTTS
1792 BLAMIRE Richard
1792–1817 SUTTON & DAVIS
1793 LAWRENCE, VULLIAMY &
   BOTT
1794 BLAMIRE Edward (no 30)
1794–5 MILLER John
1794–9 RICHDALE James
1795–9 MARTIN Leah
1798 HARBUSH & Co
1798 LUCAS & MARTIN
1799 DAVIS & SUTTON
1799 VERNON & HESSE
1806 DAMES Richard
1806 WALTON John
1811 CARLILE, LAWRENCE & Co
1813 DOORMAN, C
1815 DAMES, PAXTON & DAMES
1815–20 SUTTON & DAVIS
1817 LAWRENCE & CARLILL
1821 WALTON, FAIRBANK &
   WALTERS
1821–4 SUTTON, DAVIS & Sons
1821–34 LAWRENCE, R H & Co
1823–4 LIST John (no 30)
1823–34 PLAXTON & DAMES
1825 PLAXTON & DAVIES
1826–9 WALTON, J
1834–46 DAVIS John
1839–41 LAWRENCE Richard
   Henshaw & MORTON William
1851 DAMES Charles
1865–8 DAMES, C R & R

SHORTER STREET

1777> DIRS Carsten
<1777 HOLTHOUSE Carsten
1784–1800 DIRS & HOLTHOUSE
   (no 5)
1795 DINGWALL, J
1815–17 DIRS & MORTENS (no 5)
1823–4 HINCKEN & Co (no 1)

**ST GEORGE STREET/RATCLIFFE
HIGHWAY**

1748 KNACK & SHUTE
1765 WARRENER Jonas
1766 ELVIS John
1766–85 LUDEKEN Christopher
   (no 4)
1774 WHITEING Matthew (no 75)
1781 FILLING, A
1784 BATGER John & Son
1790s BATGER Henry & William
1792 ARMITAGE Thomas
1793 GOODHART & LAURIE

1796–1815 GOODHART, J
1811–5 BOCKEN, H C (no 2)
1814–5 GOODHART & LAURIE
   (no 4)
1821–31 GOODHART & Son
1823–4 BERG Wernert
1834 WATSON Archibald
1835 STERMICH
1840 GOODHART
1846–68 GOODHART Jacob & Son
   (nos 3–7)
1851 WACKERBARTH & COLLING
   (no 45)

ST GEORGE'S PLACE

1846–52 GRANT, BALDWIN & Co
   (no 17½)

ST MARY ST

1811–24 BALLINGER James

UPPER CHAPMAN STREET

1814–18 DETMAR David

VIRGINIA STREET

1747–9 AYRES & BROWN
1754 AIRES Jacob
1759 AYRES Jacob
1761 DIRS Cort
1762 AYRES, J
1763–6 AYRES John
1768–9 HUSON William
1770 SCHERMAN & MEYER
1777 WILLICK, G
1780 WITTICK & Co
1783–1820 DETMAR George
1790s WITTICK George & Co
1794–8 GRAVELLER & DETTMAR
1796–8 DETMAR John
1815 GAVILLER & WALES
1816 SCHULZ, J & Co
1817 GAVELLIR, G
1819 SCHULZ & LUDENORFF
1821 SCHULZ, J & Co
1830–5 HINCKEN, M & Co
1836 HOCKE, W
1839–68 HALL & BOYD

WELL STREET

1739 CARYAR, T
1747–9 STAVER, H
1752–71 ARNEY, J
1772 KRAMER, M
1789 WACKERBARTH Diederick
1790s WACKERBARTH, S & Co
1789–92 MAUDE &
   WACKERBARTH
1794–9 ARNEY & WITTE (no 13)
1794–9 MAUD & CROOK
1795 RHODE, E & M

1806 DOMOCK Baron von
1806–15 CHAMPION George Lloyd
1811 LONSDALE John (grinder)
1811–7 WAYMOUTH Fred
1813 SCHLENCKER & RICH
1816 CONSTADT
1817 ROHDE, C & Co
1817 WITTE, L&H (no 27)
1821–7 SCUDDER, G
1823–4 SMITH & DONALDSON
1826 DEMPSEY & REIS
1829–30 JONAS, H & Co
1829–31 JONAS & Son
1836 JONAS Sahle Henry

WELLCLOSE SQUARE

1724–9 MACKLEAN & IRESON
1730 MAJOR & CORDIS
1731–3 MAJOR, J
1741 CORDIS, F
1741 DARLEY, A
1746–8 DIRS, K
1747–61 RHODE, P
1747–72 RIPP, H
1748 PRITZLER, M
1749 DIRS Carsten
1749 FOLSTER, C
1750–6 TURQUAND, R & J
1751–68 BARRELL, J
1752 POITZER
1754–9 PRITZLER Mary
1754 RHODES Peter
1754–74 RIPP Henry
1758 TURQUAND, B & J
1759 ROHDE Peter
1759–66 RIPP & WHITE
1759–74 TURQUAND John
1759–79 DIRS Carsten
1759–92 ARNEY John (no 27)
1760 FRANKS & PECHERSON
1761–2 JOHNSON, C
1761–77 DIRS Cort
1762 RHODES Peter
1763 PRITZLER & Co
1763 ROLLE, A
1763–69 ROHDE Carsten & Major
1763–77 DIRS Carsten
1765 PEKERSON Dederick
1766 CLARKE, N
1766 KNIES Andrew
1766–77 HOLTZMEYER George W
   (no 35)
1767–8 BARRELL John
1768–97 KNIES & PRITZLER
1770s–1800 HOLTHOUSE Carsten &
   Christian
<1772 DOLGE Joachim Frederick
1772 MILLER & PRITZLER
1774–81 PARKER Richard (no 10)
1777 GOODHART & WILLICK

1777 WACKERBARTH, D
1778 PRITZLER, T
1781 PARKER, R & J
1781–3 PRITZLER, KNIES & ENGEL
1781–99 DIRS & HOLTHOUSE
  (no 5)
1781–94 DAVIS, W
1783 PARKER Richard & Son (no 10)
1784 WITTICK Christopher (no 30)
1784 WACKERBARTH & ARNEY
1784 WACKERBARTH & MAUD
1784–8 PELL William
1789–90s ARNEY & Co
1789–91 RHODE, C & M
1789–92 BARTHARNEY, WALKER
  & Co
1789–92 HARRISON & Co
1789–94 KNIES & PRITZLER (no 30)
1789 HOLTHOUSE & Co
1789–90 PARKER & Son (no 22)
1789–98 PRITZLER Theophilus
  (no 49)
1790s ANGELL & Co (no 49)
1791 ENGELL
1791 PELL Elizabeth
1791–98 ROHDE Carsten (no 22)
1792– PARKER Richard & Co (no 22)
1794–9 ENGEL Henry (no 48)
1794 ROHDE, C&M (no 28)
1794–6 ARNEY & WITTE (no 27)
1807–25 HUDSON & WITTE
1810 WACKERBARTH, G & JH
1811 MERTENS Lear
1811 WITTE Ludwig
1811 HARRISON William (no 54)
1811–15 WITTE, L & H (no 27)
1813–22 DOORMAN, C C
1815 ROHDE Major (no 28)
1815 DETTMAR & Co (no 30)
1815–24 TYLER John
1815–6 MARTINEAU & REID
1816–7 CONSTANT, LHHG
1816 REID, T
1816 WHITEHEAD, T
1817 DIRS & MORTENS (no 5)
1817 MARTINEAU & Co (no 48)
1820–1 MARTINEAU, D & Co
1820 SCHLENCKER & WICKE
1821 DEMPSEY & REIS
1821 SCHLENCKER, J & G
1823–4 SCHLENCKER John &
  George (no 30)
1825 HUDSON & HUNT
1825–6 HUNT, T
1829 DICKENSON William Henry
1829 SCHLENCKER & POTTER
1829–30 JONAS & HUDSON
1829–30 CHURCH & Co
1829–30 MARTINEAU & Co
1834 JONAS & Sons

1834 MARTINEAU & Sons (no 48)
1834 SCUDDER & MARMAN
  (no 30)
1836 DICKINSON, W
1851 HENRICKSON Henry
  (nos 48–49)
1865–8 BRUXNER Michael Fredrick
  (no 49)
1865–8 WAGENER John (no 27)

WENTWORTH STREET

1756 BECKMAN, N (Winkford
  Street)
1762 EGGARS, F (Winkford Street)
1766 EGNER & LEAR
1766–9 EGGERS Francis
1768–76 LEAR Margaret
1771–86 MILLS & LATER
1774–92 BRUNIGES Martin
1779 GILBERT Edward
1781–9 WACKERBARTH, Theodore
1790s BRUNIGES & ERCKS
1790–2 LATER John (no 116)
1792–6 ERCKS Henry
1796–9 BUXTON & SHALDERS
  (no 37)
1811–15 DEWS Christopher
1811–17 COSLETT Wm (no 45)
1811–17 HALTON & KURHT
1811–17 MILLER Richard
1815–17 WALKER Wm (no 66)
1823–4 COPE Geo
1829–31 MOHRMAN & Co
1830–1 MANLEY Thomas
1832 MOHRMAN & KAHRS

WHITECHAPEL ROAD

1754 ATKYNS & FLETCHER
1777–8 TURQUAND James Lewis
  (no 63)
1789–97 HOLTZMEYER George W
  (no 268)
1811 WILDE, H & J (no 268)
1813 MEINE, F (Sion Yard)
1815 WILDE Joseph (no 268)
1816–21 WAGENTRIBER & Co
  (no 268)
1819–20 BULLWINKLE &
  HOWARD (Size Yd)
1823–6 TROLLOP Henry (Size Yd)

WILLIAM STREET

1815 HAWKSWORTH, J (no 19)
1823–4 JAGER Annal Julius (no 19)

WILTSHIRE LANE

1777 WACKERBARTH, G
1779–98 WACKERBARTH George

WAPPING to LIMEHOUSE

ALBERT STREET, SHADWELL

1841–6 BROWNE Henry Nibbs
1865–8 GODBY & BOYD

BACK LANE, SHADWELL

1815 HOLEHOUSE Ann

BREWHOUSE LANE

1761–71 CAMDEN, W & J
1785 CAMDEN, LEAR &
  THELLUSON
1788–94 LEAR, HANDASYDE &
  THELLUSAN
1790–8 LEAR & HANDASYDE
1815–17 LEAR, CURTIS & Co

BROAD STREET

1728–9 HEAVISIDE, M
1731–3 SMITH & HEAVISIDE
1736–50 HEAVISIDE & WHITING
1737 WHITING, M & J
1749 SCHUTTE & KITTERRIDGE
  (Vine Street)
1771 WHITING Dorothy
1773 WHITING, D, M & J
1781 WHITING, M
1791–4 WHITING, M & J (no 75)

COAL STAIRS

1753 GOD, H
1760–2 GAY, H
1764 COOK, REINERS, DANNING
  & JOHNSON
1777–80 RICHARDSON, J (no 51)

COCK HILL

1747 WILLOUGHBY & MEYER

DEAN STREET

1771 COPE & BRODT
1777 COPE, D

EXECUTION DOCK STAIRS

1746 BACKMAN & CAMDEN

**HORSEFERRY & RIGBEYS
ROPEWALK**

1724–9 HANKIN, E (Rigbeys)
1730 BEZELY & WELFOD (Rigbeys)
1738–46 HOPPE, D (Rigbeys)
1761 OHLSON, J (Horseferry)
1771 GOODHART, E (Tites Alley)
1774–1834 GOODHART, E
  (Horseferry)
1846 GOODHART & PATRICK
1851 GOODHART, E & Son & Co
  (Horseferry)

KING DAVID LANE, SHADWELL

1846–65 MUHM, Michael (Juniper Row)

KING EDWARD'S STAIRS

1736 STEGER, H

KING JAMES'S STAIRS

1749–62 DIRS, C
1750 LEFEBURE, J
1750–2 DIRS, K

KING STREET

1761 GRIFFITHS & HYLL
1776 ARNOLD & KAMER
1817 SCHLENKER, George

LOWER SHADWELL

1789–98 GUTZMER, Henry

MILK YARD

1747 POPE, J
1749 KRUGGER, F
1762 CLARKE, N

NARROW STREET

1772–3 SMITH & SYKES
1781 LABARD, P
1792–4 HICKSON & STOWE
1798–9 HICKSON & NORTH
1815 HICKSON, E
1817 HICKSON Wm

NEW GRAVEL LANE

1811–17 SCHLENCKER George (no 144)
1821 SCHLENCKER, T
1847–94 BOSTELMANN Johann Peter (no 12)
1882 DREIER Johann (no 1)

OLD GRAVEL LANE

1767 DIRS Cort
1773–83 SARFAS Henry
1777 SLACK Thomas & Co
1785–6 BURRELL, ADAMS, CAMDEN, LEAR & THALISON
1785–92 CAMDEN, HOWARD & HENKIN
1794 CAMDEN, LEAR & THELLUSEN
1794–99 DENT, F
1817–24 ALTHEREITH, J
1818–31 NASMYTH & Co
1820 RYDER & NASMYTH

RATCLIFF CROSS

1743 RODDY, T
1768–9 WHITING & KEEN
1778–80 WHITING Matthew (no 75)

1781 SMITH, J
1790–2 LUDEKEN Christopher & Son
1808–31 STEINMETZ, W (Phoenix Place)
1834 WATSON & Co (Phoenix Place)

SHAKESPEARE WALK

1757 DIEZ & DEBELE
1763 HOMAN Julius

SILVER STREET

1793–9 KALTEISEN Casper
1815 HARBUSCH Vander
1830 HUCK, W
1831 HACKE, W
1834 HOCKER Werner

SUN TAVERN FIELDS

1796–1815 FILLING Adam

UNION STREET

1815 GOODHART & NORTH
1839 STEVENS George

WAPPING DOCK

1727–9 LORANCE, DAVIS & ROBINSON
1732 STEGER & BOSTOK
1733–5 STEGER, H
1746 BATRAM, J

WAPPING NEW STAIRS

1722–4 CORDIS, F (Warren Square)
1725 CORDIS, DAVIS, DAVIES & HARDING (Warren Square)
1728 CORDIS, F
1735 STEDDON, J
1748 BACKMAN & CAMDEN
1791–3 LEAR, HANDASYDE & THELLUSAN
1802 LEAR & HANDASYDE

WAPPING WALL

1766–9 MOXHAM James

LAMBETH to BERMONDSEY

against ARCHBISHOP'S PALACE

1733 VASTEN & KIPPLIN

BANKSIDE

1792–9 GOULDING Thomas, sugar mill maker (no 45)

CHURCH STAIRS

1752 JASTRUM, P (and Hanover Stairs)

CHURCH STREET

1756–60 JEMMITT, T

COTTONS WHARF

1819 SEVERN, KING & Co

EAST LANE

1770 GRIFFITHS, C

GRAVEL LANE

1730 MERLOTT, A

GREEN STREET

1854–1890 SMITH & TYERS (no 14)

Gt GUILDFORD STREET

1821 MYER (MAYER) John (America Street)

GULLEY HOLE

1746 TUCKWELL, W
1754 FLAGMAN, H
1762 PECKERSON & LEYNDECKER

HANOVER STAIRS

1752 JASTRUM, P (and Church Stairs)

KINGS ARMS STAIRS

1748 SCHEVE, J

MASONS STAIRS

1740–2 STEAGER, H

MILL STREET

1853 BRITISH SUGAR REFINING Co

NARROW WALL

1723 HUNT, M (Cupers Bridge)
1729 HUNT, H (Cupers Bridge)
1732 SHEVES, J (Cupers Gardens)

SNOW FIELDS

1868 HILL Adam (no 111)

ST MARY OVERSTAIRS

1734–9 MERLOTT, A

ST OLAVE STREET / TOOLEY STREET

1740 BARKER & McKINDSEY
1741 BROOKS

WEBBER ROW

1846 GAYLOR Tho (no 40)

WORCESTER STREET

1746 TURQUAND & SNEE

1749 TURQUAND, R & J

SILVERTOWN

1864–87 DUNCAN James
1865 DUNCAN, BELL & SCOTT
1878–1921 TATE Henry
1881–1921 LYLE Abram
1887–?90 MARTINEAU David
1921– present TATE & LYLE

BRISTOL

BACK STREET

1830 BURGE & CHILTON

BLACKFRIARS

1775 REES (no 1)

BRISTOL BRIDGE

1685–1720 TAYLOR
1715–30 WILLCOCKS William & Co

BRUNSWICK SQUARE

1793–4 GRAVENOR William
1793–4 PEMBER William

CASTLE STREET

1867–1906 Messrs. YOUNG, WILLS
 & Co

CATHAY

1790s KATER Henry

COUNTERSLIP

1704–36 WHITCHURCH Edward
1736–40 GARLICK Edward I
1736–81 GARLICK Edward II
1736–88 ELTON Isaac
1775 GARLICK & Co (no 7)
1775 FRENCH Samuel (no 14)
1781–88 ELTON, SANDERS & Co
1788–94 SANDERS William
1793–4 BRIGHT Henry
1793–4 FEDDEN William
1838–81 FINZEL & Co
1840 DAVIS & FINZEL

DUCK LANE

1715> COLE Lawford
<1726–28 LANE Benjamin
1728–35 GARLICK, HUNT, BARNES
1729–62 BARNES William & Co
1735–62 BRICE Samuel

GLOUCESTER STREET

1793–4 BIDDOE Thomas

GT GEORGE STREET /
TRAITORS BRIDGE

1771–90 BATTERSBY William
1775 BATTERSBY, HULL & Co
 (no 4)
1784 BATTERSBY, HARFORD &
 LUNNELL
1785–97 REILY & VAUGHAN
1793–4 REILY & Co
1803–13 MAIS & THOMAS
1813 PHILLIPS Thomas & Co

GUINEA STREET

1808 RANKIN Robert

HALLIERS LANE / BRIDEWELL
LANE / NELSON STREET

Halliers/Bridewell…
1712–75 DAUBENY George I & II
 (no 1)
1712–75 DAUBENY John (no 1)
1775–1812 DAUBENY George III &
 IV
1793–4 DAUBENEY & HARRIS
1793–4 HENDERSON Samuel & Co
1815–17 BIGGS & SAVERY
Nelson…
1775 PEACH & HENDERSON
 (no 2?)
1790–1807 HENDERSON Samuel &
 Co
1807–20 CARTWRIGHT & BEDDOE
1820–28 STANTON Daniel
1830 BLACKWELL Samuel & Jas

HOST STREET / UNDER THE
BANK

Host Street…
1790s SMITH James
1796 RANKIN Robert & Thomas
Under the Bank…
1793–4 IRELAND, WRIGHT & Co

LEWINS MEAD

1728> DAMPIER & COOMBE
1731–47 GIFFORD John
1775 RIGG Joseph, jun (no 13)
1775 BARNS (no 19)
1775 RICE (no 19)
1775 PEDEN Irner (no 20)
1793–4 HARRIS John & Sons
1793–4 MILES William & Co
1799 PARSONS & Co
1838> FINZEL & Co

MERCHANT STREET

1840 GUPPY Brothers

MONTAGUE STREET

1793–3 HARRIS John jun

OLD KING STREET

1724–41 HOOKE Abraham &
 HOULTON Joseph
1775 BOOTH CHAMPION & Co
 (no 26)
1784 BOOTH Thomas
1793–4 CARTWRIGHT, SMITH &
 BEDDOE

OLD MARKET

1704–15 WILLCOCKS William & Co
1715 HUNT, ELTON, SALMON,
 GARLICK
1726–8 GARLICK Edward II
1737–60 HUNT Samuel, jun
1763–75 BRICE Edward (no 66)
1784–94 BRICE Edward & Nathaniel
1790s BRICE Nathaniel (no 43)
1840 BRUCE, BUTTERWORTH &
 HIER
1850 HIER & STOCK (no 66)
1899–1912 BRISTOL SUGAR
 REFINERY

QUAKERS FRIARS

1784–90s GRAVENOR & Sons
1803 GRAVENOR & MAIS

QUAY HEAD

1760–1859 AMES, IRELAND & Co
1830–40 HOLDEN & VINING
<1859 FUIDGE, FRIPP & Co

RED LODGE STREET

1775 MADDOCKS John (no 4)
1775 BRIDLE Robert (no 12)
1775 WILLIAMS Rowland (no 16)

REDCLIFFE STREET

1682 BROWNE Morgan
1689–1700 HORT Isaac (Gt House)
1695–1712 NEWPORT John
1700–15 HORT Thomas (Gt House)
<1723 TYTE (no 18)
1723–50 MACIE David (no 18)
1757–75 BLOOM, BANISTER,
 HOBHOUSE & Co (no 97)
1775 MORGAN BLAKE & Co
 (no 97)
1775 KEENE Allis & Thomas
 (nos 18 & 19)
1793–4 KEENE Thomas & Son

ROSEMARY STREET

1793–4 GRAVENOR William & Sons

SMALL STREET

1790s HEMBURG Thomas

ST AUGUSTINES BACK

1653–79 KNIGHT John
1676–7 WATKINS John
1679–96 LANE Richard
1696–1704 COLE

ST JOHNS BRIDGE

1728–58 REED Edward & Son
1761–69 HENDERSON & PEACH
1770–84 RIGGE Joseph
1788–1802 MILES William &
    INGRAM James
1803–18 BAMFORD & MATTHEWS
1819–32 HOLDEN & VINING & Co

ST PETERS SUGAR HOUSE

1612–34 ALDWORTH Robert
1634–50 ELBRIDGE Giles
1650–65 CHALLONER Thomas &
    Robert
1665–1696 BEAUCHAMPE Richard

ST STEPHEN STREET

1830 BRICE, STOCK & FRY

TEMPLE BACK

1775–1805 WRIGHT John (no 10)
1790s BRIGHT Henry
1790s FEDDEN Hymer
1805–1809 WRIGHT Edward
    Brumsby (no 10)

TEMPLE STREET

1662–78 LANE Richard & HINE
    John
1679–99 HINE John
1712–23 MACIE John & Co
1723–31 DAUBENY George & Co
1731–42 PINFOLD John & Co
1774–96 BISSEX Rachael
1775 FLINN & PALMER (no 107)
1784 FLINN James

(ST) THOMAS STREET

1661 HINE John
1662–78 LANE Richard
1672–82 HINE John
1724–50 BLOOM Nicholas
1775 TANDY John & Co (no 66)
<1783 WEEKS Cordis & Co

TUCKER STREET / BATH STREET

1683 TAYLOR Richard & Co
1775 OTTO John (no 5)
1775 REINCKE John (no 6)
1775–86 KROGER Gunter Henry
    (no 15)
1790s KATER John Henry
1790s OTTO John
1793–4 KATER John & Henry

1793–4 TUCKETTS & FLETCHER

UPPER MAUDLIN LANE

1790s GRAVENOR William

WHITSON COURT

1665–82 ELLIS Thomas
1682–3 WEBB Nathaniel, POPE
    Michael & WHITING John
1683–91 POPE Michael & WHITING
    John
1691–1723 POPE Michael
1723–51 POPE
1751–75 POPE, COLLETT & Co
1775–93 MUNCKLEY, SMITH & Co
1793–1824 DIGHTON, WAIT,
    DYMOCK & Co

WILDER STREET

1754–75 COLLETT John
1775–1801 PEMBER William
1790s PEMBER, DURBIN & Co
1801–11 HEINEKIN & ORMISTON
1811–49 SAVAGE John & Francis

CHESTER

CUPPINS LANE

1755–64 WILSON Ben, HINCKS
    John, MANESTY Jos
1764–67 WILSON Ben, HINCKS
    John
1767–72 HINCKS John
1772–77 HINCKS Arbella, HINCKS
    Rbt
1777–78 HINCKS Arbella, BOULT
    Wm

SKINNERS LANE / SHIPGATE ST

1784–?1794 ROBERTS Thomas

WEAVERS LANE

1745 ??
1782–9 HESKETH Robert &
    KENNERLEY John

DUBLIN

ABBEY STREET

1780 DARCY Ann (no 187)

ASTON QUAY

1760 NAIRAC John
1780 NAIRAC & COLLINS (no 38)

COOK STREET

Mullinahack...
abt 1745–62 PAUMIER John & Peter
1760 LEESON William
1760 CONNOR John
1780 BYRNE Edward & John
1780 GEOGHEGAN & GARRETT

EARL STREET SOUTH

1844–8 JAGGERS John & WORTHS
    James

EXCHEQUER STREET

1780 TARDY & TAURON (no 12)

FADE STREET

1760 GELLIS John

FRANCIS STREET

1760 PERRIER Anthony
1780 LONG Patrick (no 106)
1780 NOWLAND Thomas (no 110)

GEORGE'S STREET

1760 BERTRAND & LESEURE
1760 MARTIN Peter

GLOUCESTER STREET SOUTH

1846–52 JAGGERS & FEREDEY

HAWKINS STREET

1760 AUDOUIN Isaac
1760 VILLEBOIS John
1780 TARDY & POMERADE (no 16)

HENRY STREET

1760 SIMON & MORIN (Cole's
    Lane)
1780 MORIN John (Cole's Lane)

KING STREET NORTH

1850 O'FLAHERTY John (no 166)

MARY'S ABBEY

1780 GALAN & MAZIERE (no 6)

MARY'S LANE

1780 CANUER John & Co (no 56)

PRINCES STREET SOUTH

1846–52 JAGGERS & FEREDEY

SKINNERS ALLEY

1760 PERRIER Anthony

STEPHEN STREET

1760 VIGNAU & DUBEDAT
1780 FIELD William (no 26)

EARLESTOWN

1855> SANKEY Sugar Works

EDINBURGH / LEITH

BREADALBANE STREET

1866–80 BONNINGTON SUGAR
REFINING Co

CANONGATE

1778–81 KAMPTIE Francis (no 160)
1829–1852 MACFIE William & Co
(no 160)

COBURG STREET

1800–60 LEITH SUGAR REFINING
Co

ELBE STREET

1804–1835> MACFIE William & Co

GLASGOW

ALSTON STREET

1809–10 WILSON & STRANG
1810> WILSON
1848 WILSON & Sons
1850s–66 WILSON, TAYLOR & Co
1866–68 WILSON, FINLAY &
SPIERS

BELL'S WYND

1778 North Sugar House

CANDLERIGG STREET

Western Sugar House…
1667–1787 ANDERSON William
1667–1787 CALDWELL John
1667–1787 CRAIG James
1667–1787 CRAIG William
1667–1787 CUMMINS Robert
1667–1787 GEMMIL Peter
1667–1787 GRAHAM John
1667–1787 GRAHAM Richard
1667–1787 HAMILTON Frederick
1667–1787 STARK John
Candleriggs…
1777–99 PHILLIPS John

GALLOWGATE

Eastern Sugar House…
1669 PEDDIE James
1669 CROSS John
1669 CROSS Robert
1669 BOGLE George

1669 LUKE John
1736 BOGLE Robert
1736 GRAHAM John
1750–99 MacNAIR Robert
1750–79 HOLMES Jean
1787–99 MacNAIR James
1799> STRANG John
1799> WILSON Samuel
1799> McLEROY John
1799> PATERSON James

HIGH JOHN STREET

1800–4 PHILLIPS John
1804–5 LOVE Hugh
1805–9 WILSON, STRANG & Co
1809–11 PHILLIPS John
1811–16 PHILLIPS Thomas
1816–18 BELL

KING STREET

Little Sugar House…
1736 GORDON William
King's Street Sugar Works…
1736 BUCHANAN Andrew
1736 COULTER John
1736 MONTGOMERY James
1736 MURDOCH Peter, sen & jun

OSWALD STREET

Ann Street…
1832–54 McEWAN & Sons
1854> KIRKLAND John & Sons
<1864 BAIRD, PATERSON & BAIRD

PORT DUNDAS

1851–69 MURDOCH & DODDRELL
Port-Dundas Sugar Refining Co…
1871–77 DODDRELL George J
1871–77 READMAN, J

QUEEN ST

<1807 McNAIR, R & J

STOCKWELL STREET

South Sugar Works…
1736 ANDERSON James
1736 McDONAL William
1736 MILLIKEN James

WASHINGTON STREET

<1830 McNAIR James
1830> REID & PEARSON
1830> KIRKLAND John & Sons
<1849 WAINWRIGHT
1864–77 JOHNSTON William

GREENOCK

BAKER STREET

1831–51 ANDERSON Alexander &
Thomas
1848–77 PATTEN Archibald & Co
1858–60s SCOTT Alex
1858–60s DUNCAN James
1858–60s BELL James
1864–66 CAMBELL
1864–66 DAWSON
1864–66 DICKSON

BOGLE STREET

1802–54 MACFIE Robert & Sons

CARTSDYKE BRIDGE

1797–1846 FAIRRIE James & Co

CLARENCE STREET

1812 CRAWFORD Hugh
1814 LEITCH William
1835 LEITCH James & William
1835 OUGHTERSON James
1844 CONNAL Ebenezer
1844–7 PARKER William

CRESCENT STREET

1851–57 WREDE & Co
1857–59 WREDE, THORNE & Co
1862–89 AITKEN James
1862–70 LANG James
1862–70 MUIR James P
1862–70 SCOTT William
1870–89 STEWART Andrew
1870–95 THORBURN James G
1889–95 PATERSON, RR

DELLINGBURN RESERVOIR

1853–65 NEILL & DEMPSTER
1858–95 ADAM William
1858–95 BALLANTINE, J H
1858–95 ROWAN Thomas B

DRUMFROCHER ROAD (1)

1852–64 ANDERSON, ORR & Co
1870s–96 SCOTT Alex & Sons
abt 1896> The BREWERS SUGAR
Co Ltd

DRUMFROCHER ROAD (2)

1868 DEMPSTER Duncan F
1868 NEILL George
1868 NEILL John

DRUMFROCHER ROAD (3)

1873–89 CAMBELL Dugald
1873–89 COWAN John
1873–89 LIVINGSTONE Alex

1873–89 NEILL Robert
1873–89 NEILL Tom
1873–89 OLIPHANT, R D

EAST HAMILTON STREET

1885> Sugar Warehouses at John
    Watt Dock

INGLESTON STREET

1847–81 BLAIR, REID & STEELE
1864–78 PAUL, SWORD & Co
1889> AITKEN James
1889> AITKEN John Crawford
1889> DOWNIE Andrew
1889> STEWART Andrew

INVERKIP STREET

1847–57 FERGUSON & Co

KER STREET

1831–36 YOUNG Thomas
1845–1858 FAIRRIE James & Co
1858–65 DAVIE John
1858–65 MACKERDY, L
1858–65 STEELE David
1865 GRIEVE James J & Walter
1865 HUNTER Charles P
1865 KERR John
1865 LYLE Abram
1865–1876 HUNTER
1865–1882 LYLE
1865–1900> KERR
1865–1900> GRIEVE

MAIN STREET

1847–48 PARKER Matthew

PORT GLASGOW ROAD

1833–41 SPEIRS & WREDE
1845–59 SPEIRS James
1859–77 ANDERSON, A A

PRINCES STREET

1826–38 ANGUS Alexander & Co
1838–43 MacLEISH, KEYSER & Co
1843–48 PATTEN Archibald & Co
1848–96 WALKER John & Co
1928> WALKER John & Co

**ROBERT STREET, PORT
GLASGOW**

<1869 FOWLER

ROXBURGH STREET

1832 HUTTON Hugh & Co
1839–45 CONNAL & PARKER

SHAWS WATER

1829–37 TASKER, YOUNG & Co
1837–1839 FAIRRIE James & Co

1840s–51 WREDE & Co
1855 CRAWHILL, SCHULTZ & Co
1870s CRAWHILL, ALLISON & Co
1878> HOGG
1878> WALLACE

SUGAR HOUSE LANE (1)

1765 ALEXANDER Claud
1765 CONNELL Arthur
1765 DUNLOP Thomas
1765 HOPKIRK Thomas
1765 MacCUNN William
1765 WHITE Archibald
1765 WILSON Alex
1765 KUHLL Mark
1812 HOPKIRK James
1812 MACKENZIE Daniel & James
<1831 ATHERTON, MACKELLAR
    & Co
<1840 McCALLUM Duncan
1843–6 BLANKEN Harm & Co
1846–54 FAIRRIE James & Co
1854 HOYLE MARTIN & Co
1870–79 GIBB Duncan Hoyle
1870–79 GIBB John Hoyle
1879–82 ADAM Robert George &
    William
1879–82 MacEACLRAN Douglas
1885–1921 KERR Robert

SUGAR HOUSE LANE (2)

1788 WILSON John
1788 RITCHIE Walter
1788 ROBERTSON George
1788 RAMSEY Thomas
1788 MacCUNN William
1788 HUNTER James
1788–1800 MACFIE Robert
1800 HUNTER, MACALPINE & Co
1800> MACKELLAR Duncan
1815 ANGUS Alexander
1829–43 MacLEISH, KEYSER & Co
1847 HOYLE MARTIN & Co
1870–86 CURRIE Alexander & Co

HULL

CHURCH STREET

1798?–1817 BOYES, G F & Co

LIME STREET

1732–1840 THORNTON, WATSON
    & Co

SOUTH END

Abt 1660 sugarhouse

TRIPPET

1658–<1673 SMITH William &
    CATLIN William

WINCOLMLEE

1790–8 BASSANO, CARLILL & Co

LANCASTER

ST LEONARDS GATE

<1684 HODGSON John
1684 LAWSON John
1746 LAWSON Rbt, HARGREAVES
    Hy, ASTLEY Luke
1760 LAWSON Rbt, HARGREAVES
    Hy, ASTLEY Luke + 3
<1766 FOXCROFT Rbt
1766–9 LAWSON Rbt, RAWLINSON
    Abraham, HARGREAVES Hy,
    ASTLEY Luke, BIRKETT Miles,
    FOXCROFT Geo
1769–72 LAWSON Rbt,
    RAWLINSON Abraham,
    HARGREAVES Hy, ASTLEY
    Luke
1772–3 LAWSON Rbt, RAWLINSON
    Abraham, HARGREAVES Hy
1784 LAWSON, RAWLINSON & Co
1790s HARGREAVES James
1828–34 CROSFIELD George & Co

LIVERPOOL

ARGYLE STREET

<1769 sugarhouse

BACHELOR STREET

<1841 WAINWRIGHT &
    GADESDEN
1841–1870s MACFIE
1841–1938 MACFIE & Sons
1872 MACFIE & Co
1875 POPE Luke

BLACK DIAMOND STREET

1840s–1850s JAGAR George with Mr
    Manisty
1872 JAGER George & Co

BLACKSTOCK STREET

1852?–1872 LEITCH James & Co
    (no 14)
1853?–1872 CROSSFIELD Edward &
    Co (no 20)

BLUNDELL STREET

1816–29 MORTON William (no 72)

BURLINGTON STREET

1872 JAGER George & Co (no 77)

CASTLE STREET

1766 TARLETON John & Co
1784 TARLETON & Co

CHISENHALE STREET

1828–9 MORGENSTERN Henry & Son

COOK STREET

<1760 HUGHES John
1899 BOSTOCK & Co

DALE STREET

1766 BLUNDELL Jonathan & Co
1816–7 BYROM Henry (no 15)
1828–9 MOLLENHAUER J H (no 47)
1923 STEEL, W Harvey & Co, Merchants (no 62)

DICKENSON STREET

1832 SHERLOCK, J C

DUKE STREET

1766 CAMPBELL George, FENN & Co

EARLE STREET

1860 TATE Henry & Sons

ELDON PLACE

1832 VICCARS John

GT GEORGE STREET

1864 SCHULTZ Henry

GREENLAND STREET

1816–7 ERCKS Henry (no 52)
1824–5 MORGENSTERN & MOLLENHAUER (no 57)

HARRINGTON STREET

1784 WATERWORTH & Co
1824–5 DOWNWOOD & MANN (no 43)
1824–9 BUGGELN Luhr (no 27)
1828–9 DOWNWARD & RYLAND (no 43)

JOHN STREET

1766 KNIGHT John & Co
1766 HUGHES Richard & Co
1816–7 NOBLE & HARVEYS

LOVE LANE

1869–1921 TATE Henry & Sons (no 12)
1921–1981 TATE & LYLE

MANISTY LANE

1809> WRIGHT John
1859–1866 TATE Henry & WRIGHT John

MATTHEW STREET

1766 GILDART, RAUTHMEL & Co
1816–7 DOWNWARDS & MANN
1816–29 BRANCKER & Co (no 39)
1832 EVANS Thomas

NAYLOR STREET

1843 MOLLENAUR Henry

OLD DOCK

First sugarhouse in Sugar House Yard

OLD HALL STREET

1824–5 MORGENSTERN & MOLLENHAUER (no 14)
1828–9 THORNHILL William
1828–9 TORICK Henry John (Barton's Lane)
1828–9 WEBB & MEHRTENS

OLDHAM STREET

1816–7 DAVIES & WEBB

PARLIAMENT STREET

1816–7 DISTEL & Co
1832 SUMMERFIELD William P

RAINFORD SQUARE

1816–7 HOLMES, A J & J

REDCROSS STREET

1673 SMITH, CLEIVELAND & DANVERS
1766 OLDHAM, CALDWELL & Co
1766 WAKEFIELD Thomas & Co

ST JAMES ST

1828–9 ERCKES Henry (no 10)

TEMPLE STREET

1800?–1829 HUTCHINSON William (no 1)
1828–9 SUMMERFIELDS & LENTON
1838–1872 MACFIE & Sons
1838 MACFIE

UPPER POWNALL STREET

1860?–1872 HEAP Joseph & Sons

VAUXHALL ROAD

1835 RING
1847–1866 FAIRRIE, J T & A
1853–1872 CROSSFIELD, BARROW & Co (no 32)
1866–1929 FAIRRIE & Co Ltd (no 253)
1899 CRIDDLE William E (no 245)

VERNON STREET

1872 MACFIE & Co

WAPPING

1828–9 ERCKES Henry (no 21)

WELLINGTON STREET / ELLENBOROUGH ST

1852?–1872 LEITCH James & Co

WILLIAM STREET

1841 MACFIE
1846–1872 MACFIE & Sons

MANCHESTER

CANNON STREET

1854–72 SHARP & GALLOWAY (no 1)
1888 BATES, T & Co (Liverpool) (no 14)

CHAPEL STREET

Middleton's Court
1854–88 SHARP & GALLOWAY

CHATHAM STREET SUGAR WORKS, Chorlton on Medlock

1881 "UNINHABITED" in census

CHESTER STREET

1850–4 BINYON & SHAPLAND (no 4)
1855–61 BINYON & FRYER (no 1)
1863–72 FRYER, BENSON & FOSTER

CORPORATION STREET

1874–91 SHARP & GALLOWAY (no 94)
1886 BUDGETT James & Son (no 51)

FENNEL STREET

1886 WILKINSON William (merchant) (no 31)

GARTSIDE STREET

1891 DUCHE T, M & Sons (glucose) (no 14)

Gt ANCOATS STREET

1868–9 HARRISON John (no 86)

LOWER MOSELEY STREET

1868–9 AULD James (no 18)

NEW WAKEFIELD STREET

1865 FRYER, BENSON & FOSTER

OXFORD STREET

1846 BINYON & SHAPLAND
1852 SHARP & SCOTT (no 93)
1853 SIMKINS & CROOKELL
1855–6 SMITH Geo Hugh (no 93)

PORTLAND STREET

1888 HOONINGHANS J (no 34?)
1891 HOENINGHAUS, J (glucose)
  (no 54)

POTTS STREET, ANCOATS

1858 SHARP, W

WARWICK STREET

1868–9 CALLON, T & W (no 20)

WATER STREET

1772 NORCAT Samuel
1772 RYLONE Thomas
1777 NORCOTT Samuel
1788 SUGAR BAKING COMPANY

NEWCASTLE upon TYNE

QUAYSIDE

1778 ATKINSON & Co

THE CLOSE

1778 FORSTER & Co

1787 FORSTER, RANKIN & ATKINSON
1795 FORSTER Joseph
1801 RANKIN & WATSON
1811 DOUBLEDAY & EASTERBY

NEWCASTLE-under-LYME

LONDON ROAD

<1881> VICTORIA SUGAR REFINERY

PLYMOUTH

MILL LANE / MILL STREET

1830s BRYANT & JAMES (Mill Lane)
1838–56 BRYANT & BURNELL (Mill Lane)
1851 BENSON Gerd & John (Mill Street Sugar House)
1851 BRYANT James, jun. (Mill Street Sugar House)
1890 BATES, Sir Edward

MOUNT GOULD ROAD

1750 First Sugar House

SHEFFIELD

COALPIT LANE

1737–88 BENNET Edward

EFFINGHAM LANE

1862 GREAVES Samuel (Bacon Island)

EXCHANGE STREET

1852 WALKER & WALL
1862 WALKER, G & Son

NURSERY STREET

1828–41 REVELL Samuel & Co (no 33)
<1842 VON HOLLEN John

SOUTHAMPTON

CANUTE ROAD

1847–82 GARTON, HILL & Co

SUGAR HOUSE LANE

1740s–1774 BRISSAULT John

WARRINGTON

SUGAR HOUSE LANE / RIDING STREET

<1778 PATTEN Thomas & LEIGH John
1778–81 PARR Joseph, HESKETH Robert & ASTLEY Richard
1781 LYON Thomas
1781–4 PARR Joseph

WHITEHAVEN

DUKE STREET

1712 LOWTHER, Sir James
1821 JOHNSON & MANLEY
1829 JOHNSON Edward & Co

SCOTCH STREET

1829 JOHNSTON Edward (no 4)

Appendix 4
Reading List

Sugar Refining – The Trade and The People

History of Sugar (2vols), by Noel Deerr, London: Chapman & Hall. 1949–50.

Notes on the Sugar Industry of the United Kingdom, by John M. Hutcheson, James McKelvie & Son, Greenock, 1901.

Sugar Refining Families of Great Britain, by G. Fairrie, London: Tate & Lyle, 1951.

Sugar, by Fairrie, Liverpool: Fairrie & Co., 1925.

The Plaistow Story, by Oliver Lyle, Tate & Lyle Ltd, 1960.

Sugar and All That: a History of Tate & Lyle, by Antony Hugill, Gentry Books, 1978. ISBN 0 85614 048 1.

Sugar – A Handbook for Planters & Refiners, by Charles Lock, Benjamin Newlands & John Newlands, pub. E. & F. N. Spon, London, 1888.

Die Zuckerbäcker waren vornehmlich Hannoveraner, by Horst Rössler, 2003.

The London Sugar Refiners around 1800, by Walter M. Stern, Guildhall Miscellany No 3, 1954.

A Day at a Sugar Refinery, by G. Dodd, The Penny Magazine No 582, April 1841.

The Useful Arts & Manufactures of Gt Britain – Sugar, Soc. of Promoting Christian Knowledge, 1846.

Essex and Sugar, by Frank Lewis, Phillimore & Co Ltd, 1976. ISBN 0 85033 107 2.

Sugar, by Martineau & Eastick, Pitman, 1938.

The Story of Sugar, by L. A. G. Strong, Weidenfeld & Nicolson, 1954.

Henry Tate 1819–1899, by Tom Jones, Tate & Lyle, 1960.

Tate & Lyle Times – Visitors Edition, circa 1955.

Sugar, by J. A. C. Hugill, Cosmo Pub and Tate & Lyle, 1949.

Mr Cube's Roots, Tate & Lyle.

1855–1955: A hundred years of progress – Manbré and Garton Ltd, by John L. Garbutt, 1955.

Manbré: A hundred years of sugar refining in Hammersmith, 1874–1974, by Jeanne Stoddard, Fulham & Hammersmith Hist. Soc., 1974.

Chronicles of Cannon Street: A few records of an old firm – Joseph Travers and Sons Limited, 1957.

The Story of Czarnikow, by Hurford Janes & H. J. Sayers, Harley, 1963.

Bristol's Sugar Trade and Refining Industry, by Donald Jones, Bristol Branch of the Historical Association, The University, Bristol, 1996. ISBN 0 901388 78 5.

Bristol & Gloucestershire Archaeological Society – Transactions Vols 65, 68, 74, 76, 80, 84, 85.

A Hundred Years of Sugar Refining (Love Lane Refinery 1872–1972) (Liverpool), by J. A. Watson, Tate & Lyle Ltd, 1973.

Sweetness and Power, by Sidney W. Mintz, Penguin, 1986. ISBN 0 14 00.9233 1.

Sugar – the Grass that Changed the World, by Sanjida O'Connell, Virgin Books, 2004. ISBN 1 85227 034 9.

Art de Rafiner le Sucre by Duhamel du Monceau (1764), pub. Connaissance et Memories Europeennes, 2000. (in French)

L'Industrie du Sucre by Louis Figuier, pub. Comedit, 1995. ISBN 2 909 112 35 7. (in French)

Technology for Sugar Refinery Workers, by Oliver Lyle, Chapman & Hall, 1957.

Tales of a Sugar Tramp, by Emile C. Freeland, Pelican Publishing Co, 1954.

For younger readers

Sticky Jam – The Story of Sugar, by Meredith Hooper, pub. Walker Books, 2003. ISBN 0 7445 8301 2.

Let's Learn about Sugar, by Maud & Miska Petersham, pub. Harvey House, NY, 1969.

A Sweet Surprise – (a tour of a Louisiana sugarcane mill), by Pamela Folse, 1995.

Bristol and the Sugar Trade, by Alison Grant, Longman, 1981. ISBN 0 582 21724 5.

History of the Locations

The A-Z of Regency London, The London Topographical Soc. No 131, 1985. ISBN 0 902087 19 3. (Excellent maps, including house numbers, by Horwood around 1812… one of a series of books of maps of different periods.)

Topography of London, by John Lockie, London Topographical Society, 1994. (A facsimile of John Lockie's Gazetteer 1813). ISBN 0 902087 39 8. (A must for "London" researchers)

The Godfrey Edition of Old Ordnance Survey Maps, Alan Godfrey Maps. (Available for most locations)

Dr. Johnson's London, by Liza Picard, Weidenfeld & Nicolson, 2000. ISBN 0 297 84218 8.

London: The German Connection, by Kay Mann, KT Publishing, 1993. ISBN 0 9522380 0 4.

The London Encyclopaedia, ed. by Weinreb & Hibbert, Book Club Associates, 1983.

London Lanes, by Alan Stapleton, Bodley Head, 1930.

London Alleys Byways & Courts, by Alan Stapleton, Bodley Head, 1925.

A History of Tower Hamlets, by Colm Kerrigan, Tower Hamlets Community Services, 1982. ISBN 0 902385 06 2.

East End 1888, by William J. Fishman, Gerald Duckworth & Co Ltd, London, 1988. ISBN 0 7156 2174 2.

The East End of London, by Millicent Rose, The Cresset Press, London, 1951.

Silvertown – An East End Family Memoir, by Melanie McGrath, Fourth Estate, 2002. ISBN 1 84115 142 4.

The Small House in Eighteenth Century London by Peter Guillery, pub. Yale Univ. Press. ISBN 0 300 10238 0.

Researching London's Houses by Colin Thom, pub. Historical Publications, 2005. ISBN 1 905286 00 7.

Liverpool – Our City, Our Heritage, by Freddy O'Connor, Bluecoat Press, 1990. ISBN 0 9516188 0 6. (Superb !)

Liverpool – It all came tumbling down, by Freddy O'Connor, Brunswick Press, 1986. ISBN 0 9509801 2 9.

Plymouth: A New History, 1603 to the Present Day, by Crispin Gill, Vol 2.

Lancaster – A History, by Andrew White, Phillimore, 2003. ISBN 1 86077 244 7.

Life in Georgian Lancaster, by Andrew White, Carnegie Publishing, 2004. ISBN 1 85936 102 1.

The Port of Bristol 1848–84, ed by David Large, Bristol Record Soc., 1984. ISBN 0 901583 05 1.

Migration

Die Zuckerbäcker waren vornehmlich Hannoveraner, by Horst Rössler, 2003.

Immigrants and Aliens, by Roger Kershaw & Mark Pearsall, PRO, 2000. ISBN 1 873162 94 4.

Bloody Foreigners, by Robert Winder, Abacus, 2005. ISBN 0 349 11566 4.

Slave Trade

Sugar & Slaves (English West Indies 1624–1713), by Richard S. Dunn, Jonathan Cape, 1973 (originally Univ. of N. Carolina Press, 1972). ISBN 0 224 00814 5.

The Slave Trade (1440–1870), by Hugh Thomas, Picador, 1997. ISBN 0 330 35437 x.

Knibb, "the Notorious", Slaves' missionary 1803–1845, by Philip Wright, Sidgwick & Jackson, 1973. ISBN 0 283 97873 3.

The Diligent – A Voyage through the Worlds of the Slave Trade, by Robert Harms. ISBN 0465028713.

Refined White, by Michael Berry, pub. by Australian Sugar Industry Museum, 2000. ISBN 0 9596395 3 5.

Sugar Spices and Human Cargo – An Early Black History of Greenwich, by Joan Anim-Addo, 1996. ISBN 0 904 399 21 4.

Insurance

Phoenix Assurance & the Development of British Insurance (2 vols), by Clive Trebilcock, CUP, 1985. ISBN 0 521 25414 0.

Things Phoenix 1782–1982, by K. B. Croker, Penshurst Press, 1982.

Indexes of the Fire Insurance Policies of the Sun Fire Office and the Royal Exchange Assurance, 1775–87, by D. T. Jenkins (booklet and set of fiche).

Fire Insurance Records for family & local historians 1696 to 1920, by David T. Hawkings, pub. by Francis Boutle, 2003. ISBN 1 903427 14 2.

Genealogy

Ancestral Trails, by Mark D. Herber, Sutton Pub., 2000. ISBN 0-7509-2484-5.

An Introduction to Tracing Your German Ancestors, by Peter Towey, FFHS, 2nd edition, 2002, ISBN 1 86006 140 0.

Surnames Index

(Not including Appendices 3 & 4)

THE COST

On 6 June 2002, I was offered the opportunity to bid for the privilege of opening a new refinery. The e-mail read… "To all Sugar Refiners. A prospective sugar refinery project in southern Philippines is available. Estimated project cost is US$300 Million. Please reply for more details. First come first served."

I wonder what the start-up cost of 12 Church Street was nearly 200 years earlier?

General Index

Acknowledgements

The website and the book go hand in hand – without the website there'd be no book, without the book I would not be able to express, in print rather than temporary electronic media, my thanks to all those who have encouraged, criticized and contributed towards the website.

The continuous prompting and encouragement from Thomas Fock and the regular exchange of information between Horst Rössler and myself have been invaluable… my thanks to my friends in Germany.

I should like to thank Lynda Whybrow, Jane E Tutte Mayberry, Paul Steinmetz and David Parr for allowing me to use their valued family pictures and documents to illustrate this book, and also the Cambridge & County Folk Museum, the McLean Museum & Art Gallery, Greenock, and the Northamptonshire Record Office, which holds the excellent Holthouse of Hellidon collection, for the use of their pictures. I have used information from a variety of archives for which I am grateful, but wish to thank specifically the City Archives in Hull, the Bristol Record Office, Cheshire and Chester Archives & Local Studies and the Southampton Museum of Archaeology for their considerable help during my visits.

Contributions large and small from researchers worldwide continually add to the information available on the website, and my thanks must go in particular to Ian Rathjen, Charles Schmalz, Robert James, Christiane Swinbank, Peter Towey, Donald Jones, Neville King, Ann Peal, Thomas Schmidt and Kim of Bristol for their research and assistance, which has helped greatly with the preparation of this book.

Author

Having found a sugar refining German ancestor, the third thing I did after joining AGFHS was to purchase their Sugar-Bakers' booklet. I can clearly remember sitting reading it whilst manning my display of framed photographs at a craft fair at a small public school in the beautiful countryside where the borders of Northamptonshire, Leicestershire and Rutland meet… little did I know that some years later I'd be writing a new one.

To justify the time spent on my unsuccessful research into Herman Almeroth's past, I collected all references to sugarbakers that I came across. This became a small database, which then went online and grew into the useful research tool it now is, and will, hopefully, continue to grow.

When I tell people the occupation I research, a puzzled look comes over their faces – they just can't understand why on earth I'd want to do it. If it hadn't been for the distant family involvement I would never have started, but although I'm absolutely no closer to finding Herman's birthplace I wouldn't dream of stopping now, there's still so much to do.

Born and bred in the north of Buckinghamshire, with parents from Hull and Dagenham, I spent my schooldays always having to explain that my first name was spelt with a "Y", my second name was "Johnson", my surname was pronounced "More" but not spelt like it, and my Mum's maiden name was "Almeroth", a name nobody had ever heard before. I spent my college years enjoying things, then worked as a teacher of design subjects at a local secondary school. A small photography business came next and I'm now a genealogist for Northamptonshire.

If my life was in reverse, I'd arrive at school able to explain that my middle name was the maiden name of my paternal great grandmother, that my surname is actually very common in Lincolnshire, and that Almeroth is German and came over here in the late 1700s… and I'd be able to show this book to a succession of exasperated English teachers!

Married with two children, both of whom have left home, and a wife who probably will if I mention the word "sugarbakers" once more!

Bryan Mawer, May 2006.

* * *

**I'm afraid I've not been able to include everybody and everything in this book.
The database, articles, maps, wills, etc. on my website get just a little closer
to that objective, but there's still a very, very long way to go.
The website is updated regularly, and new information is always gratefully accepted.**

Good luck with your research. I hope this has helped.

* * *